Stefan Bugow

Truck Scheduling
for Parcel Hubs
with Limited Conveyor
Capacities

Acknowledgements

This dissertation is the result of my work at the Institute of Production Management at Leibniz University Hannover. I would like to express my deep gratitude to all those that supported me during this time with their valuable inputs, encouragement and assistance.

Foremost, I would like to thank my supervisor Prof. Dr. Stefan Helber for his guidance, trust and insightful suggestions. He gave me the opportunity to freely pursue my research endeavours and enabled my personal and professional growth during my time at the Institute of Production Management. Further, I would like to thank Prof. Dr. Stefan Bock, head of the chair for Business Computing and Operations Research of Bergische Universität Wuppertal, for providing the second review of the thesis. I would also like to express my appreciation to Prof. Dr. Nils Foege of the Institute of Interdisciplinary Industrial Science at Leibniz University Hannover for assuming the chairmanship of the defense committee and to Dr. Michael Milde for his advisory role during the defense.

I want to express my deepest thanks to Dr. Carolin Kellenbrink who supported me as my co-supervisor. Her guidance and patient supervision helped me from the first research steps through many ups and downs and finally led to a successful joint publication in the end.

I am very thankful to Dr. Insa Südbeck and Dr. Fabian Friese for proofreading the initial version of this book and providing their input. Their critical remarks and valuable comments gave me with the opportunity to significantly improve this work.

A special thanks also goes out to all colleagues at the Institute of Production Management, who I have tremendously enjoyed working with. I will look back fondly to the animated discussions during coffee breaks, exciting visits to international conferences, joint cooking sessions and relaxing picnics in the park. Even in the tougher times throughout the pandemic they managed to keep me on track with joint sessions on the Discord voice servers and other online activities. Here, I would like to express my special appreciation for Dr. Insa Südbeck and Justine Broihan with whom I started the final phase of the research project at about the same time. I do not think that I would have been able to finish the project as smoothly without their positive encouragement and always lending a sympathetic ear when needed. Further, I would like to thank Dr. André Schnabel for being such a great office colleague during our shared time at the Institute of Production Management. My thanks also go out to my former colleagues Dr. Fabian Friese, Luise-Sophie Hoffmann, Ariane Kayser, Martin Klingebiel, Inka Nozinski, Niklas Pöch, Dr. Steffen Rickers, Dr. Cinna Seifi and Sebastian Wegel. They will always have a special place in my heart.

Finally, I am forever thankful to my family and friends for supporting me during this important period of my life. Without their kind support and backing this work would not have been possible.

Hannover
January 2023

Stefan Bugow

Contents

Acronyms

CDAP	Cross Dock Assignment Problem
FCFS	First Come First Served
FRCPSP	Resource-Constrained Project Scheduling Problem with flexible Resource Profiles
LP	Linear Program
LTT	less-than-truckload
NP	nondeterministic polynomial time
PHSP-LCC-flex	Parcel Hub Scheduling Problem with Limited Conveyor Capacities and Flexible Unloading Speeds
PHSP-LCC-fix	Parcel Hub Scheduling Problem with Limited Conveyor Capacities and Fixed Unloading Speeds
PHSP-LCC	Parcel Hub Scheduling Problem with Limited Conveyor Capacities

Symbols

α	parcel destination heterogeneity factor
at_j	arrival time of inbound j
β	gate scarcity factor
bl_o	total number of parcels in outbound o
C_{max}	schedule length
C_λ	completion time of λ
$conv_k$	current utilization of conveyor k
$\overline{d}_\lambda$	deadline of type λ
d_i	unloading duration of inbound i
di_m	length of interval m
dl_o^{max}	last deadline
dl_o	deadline of outbound truck o
dp_p	unloading duration of parcel p
$EL(t^c)$	events e in event list at time t^c
ES_u	earliest starting time at gate u
$g, u \in G$	set of inbound gates/doors
$i, j \in \mathcal{I}$	inbound trucks $\mathcal{I} = \{1, \dots, I\}$
$i \in \mathcal{I}_t \subseteq \mathcal{I}$	inbound trucks i available in period t with $\mathcal{I}_t = \{at_i, \dots, T\}$
$i \in J_t \subseteq \mathcal{I}$	available inbound trucks in period t
$k \in \mathcal{K}$	conveyor belts $\mathcal{K} = \{1, \dots, K\}$
λ	parameter reference type
l_i	number of parcels in inbound truck i
lk_{ik}	number of parcels in inbound truck i designated for conveyor k
L_{max}	maximum lateness
$load_i$	current loading status of inbound i
lr_{ik}	rate of parcels in inbound truck i designated for conveyor k per period

λ^{RK}	random key representation of a solution
$m \in \mathcal{M}$	intervals $\mathcal{M} = \{1, \ldots, M\}$
$MJ_i \subseteq \mathcal{M}$	available intervals for inbound truck i
$N_t \subseteq \mathcal{M}$	active intervals at period t
μ	deadline distribution factor
$M^- \subseteq \mathcal{M}$	subset of intervals ending before the last deadline
N	population size
$o \in \mathcal{O}$	outbound trucks $\mathcal{O} = \{1, \ldots, O\}$
$o \in O_k \subseteq \mathcal{O}$	subset of outbound trucks connected by conveyor belt k
$O_i^{sub} \subseteq \mathcal{O}$	random subset of outbound trucks
oc_g	status of gate g
p	standard processing time
$PA(t^c)$	parking lot status at time t^c
pc_k	remaining share of parcels for conveyor k
p_j	processing time of inbound j
$\overline{p}$	maximum processing time
pos_i	position of inbound truck i
pu_o	remaining share parcels for outbound o
$\underline{p}$	minimum processing time
q	uniformly distributed random number from the interval $[0, 1]$
r_k	capacity of conveyor k
r_k^{LB}	lower bound for the conveyor capacity
rt_{kt}	current utilization of conveyor k in period t
$s \in S$	shipments
σ	conveyor scarcity factor
seq	decoded truck sequence from random key representation of a solution
seq^l	parcel unloading sequence
$ship_{io}$	parcels for outbound truck o in inbound truck i
S_{max}	maximum inventory
S_λ	stored quantities of λ
$start_i^*$	optimized starting time for inbound i
st_m	starting period of interval m
$ST(t^c)$	system state at time t^c
$t, \tau \in \mathcal{T}$	periods $\mathcal{T} = \{1, \ldots, T\}$
$t \in T_i \subseteq \mathcal{T}$	periods available for inbound truck i with $\mathcal{T}_i = \{at_i, \ldots, T\}$

$\bar{t}$	time limit
t^c	current time
t^e	time of event e
t_{io}	transfer time from inbound i to outbound o
T_λ	tardiness of λ
T^{norm}	standard planning horizon length
U	number of inbound doors
U^{LB}	lower bound for the number of gates
u'	gate with the earliest starting time
uf_{ito}	number of duly parcels for outbound truck o if inbound truck i is scheduled at period t
U_λ	number of tardy outbound trucks $\lambda = o$ or shipments $\lambda = s$
um_{mo}	percentage of duly parcels for outbound truck o if an inbound truck is scheduled in interval m
w_λ	value/weight of λ
wl_{kt}	workload on conveyor k at period t
$x_{it} \geq 0$	number of parcels unloaded in period t from inbound truck i
$x_{it}^{re} \geq 0$	number of parcels unloaded in period t from inbound truck i in reduced LP
x_{it}^{share}	share of parcels unloaded in period t from inbound truck i
x_{it}^{up}	maximum number of parcels unloaded in period t from inbound truck i in fixed schedule
x_i^{min}	minimum number of parcels unloaded each period from inbound truck i
x_i^{max}	maximum number of unloaded parcels each time period from inbound truck i
y_{it}	$= \begin{cases} 1, & \text{if inbound truck } i \text{ is scheduled in period } t \\ 0, & \text{otherwise} \end{cases}$
z_i^{start}	starting time of inbound i
z_i^{end}	ending time of inbound i
z_{im}	$= \begin{cases} 1, & \text{if inbound truck } i \text{ is assigned to interval } m \\ 0, & \text{otherwise} \end{cases}$

z_{it} $= \begin{cases} 1, & \text{if inbound truck } i \text{ is at a door in period } t \\ 0, & \text{otherwise} \end{cases}$

Algorithms

Figures

Tables

1. Introduction

1.1. Subject and objective of the thesis

In recent years, the parcel delivery industry has emerged as an important part of the logistics market and exceeded a global market volume of 500 billion $ in 2020 for the first time.[1] Its growth can be attributed to developments in the e-commerce market in particular which exhibited an annual growth of over 20% in the period from 2017 to 2019.[2] Accordingly, parcel service providers are confronted with the complex task of managing large quantities of shipments for customers with a desire for fast deliveries, reliability and sustainability in the transportation process.[3] Hence, a fast, reactive and efficient supply chain is vital to organize the delivery process.

To meet these demands, distribution networks in the parcel delivery industry are mostly organized in hub-and-spoke networks. Here, smaller parcel shipments are consolidated into full truckloads in central hubs to allow for economies of scale since the transportation costs per truck are shared among a multitude of shipments.[4] Contrary to traditional warehouses, shipments from the incoming inbound trucks are usually directly transferred to outgoing outbound trucks in these hubs. The synchronization of incoming and outgoing trucks circumvents or reduces additional costs for additional tasks such as storing and order-picking of the shipments.[5] In the parcel delivery industry, outbound trucks usually leave the hub at fixed predefined deadlines to avoid delays in later stages of the network.[6] The operations inside the hub such as unloading, sorting, transferring and loading have a significant impact on the overall performance of the distribution network as all shipments have to pass

---

[1] Apex Insight (2021).
[2] eMarketer (2022).
[3] Savelsbergh and Van Woensel (2016, p. 580).
[4] Boysen et al. (2017, p. 723).
[5] Wolff et al. (2021, p. 1).
[6] Boysen et al. (2013, p. 481).

through a consolidation terminal. In the case of consolidation terminals in the parcel delivery industry, the internal transport is mostly conducted using automated conveyor systems that have finite capacity. Here, each parcel has a predefined path through the hub from the inbound gate it is unloaded from to the outbound gate it is designated for. Congestion on the hubs conveyor system can lead to a significant increase of the transfer time and thus to delays at later stages of the distribution network.[7] A schematic overview of the considered type of parcel hub in U-shape is illustrated in Figure 1.1.

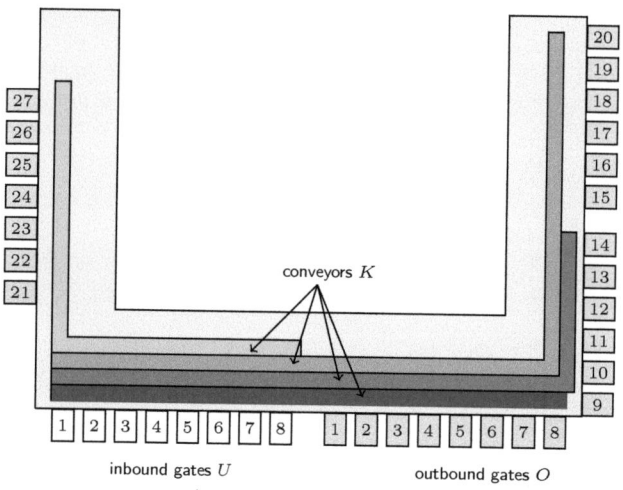

Figure 1.1.: Schematic layout of a parcel hub with conveyor network with line configuration

As the workload on the conveyors is mainly influenced by the currently unloaded inbound trucks, a potent tool to avoid congestion inside the hub is to schedule inbound trucks accordingly. Further, allowing flexibility in the unloading process is another promising measure to influence the workload and thus increase the efficiency of the hub. This dissertation seeks to address the truck scheduling problem at parcel hubs and especially focuses on how to efficiently utilize the conveyor capacities inside the hub. The conveyor capacities are explicitly considered and flexibility in the unloading process is allowed to improve the utilization of this scarce

---

[7]McWilliams et al. (2005, p. 394).

resource. As this perspective on truck scheduling at parcel hubs has not been taken yet, the dissertation aims to close the research gap.

1.2. Structure of the thesis

The second chapter illustrates the fundamentals of handling parcels in these hubs by addressing the general function as well as their physical structure. As parcel hubs are frequently organized as so called cross docks, the specifics of the distribution networks using cross docks are described and relevant planning problems on a strategic, tactical and operational level are introduced. Cross docks utilized as parcel hubs are subject to the particularities of parcel transport. Thus, the focus lies on discussing the influence of handling small shipments with a fixed destinations and strict deadlines with conveyors as means of internal transport on the structure and operation of the parcel hub.

The third chapter concentrates on the inbound truck scheduling problem at cross docks in general and outlines a classification framework of particular problem settings based on the objective, operational and gate characteristics. On the basis of the classification scheme, the truck scheduling problem at parcel hubs is defined and relevant literature discussed. Additionally, the novel extension of allowing controllable unloading speed of inbound trucks is introduced.

The fourth chapter formally introduces mathematical models for the **P**arcel **H**ub **S**cheduling **P**roblem with **L**imited **C**onveyor **C**apacities (PHSP-LCC). Firstly, basic assumptions are defined and the fundamentals of two modeling approaches are explained, namely a time-based and an interval-based approach. For the two basic modelling approaches, both a mixed integer program excluding flexibility and one including flexibility in the unloading process are presented, respectively. The notation and assumptions of each model are presented and a formal definition of the model and an explanation of the constraints follows. Further, each formulation is implemented for an exemplary instance of the problem setting and solved with the standard solver Gurobi. The results are illustrated with regard to the resulting truck schedule and conveyor utilization. The chapter also includes a proof of the NP-hardness of the problem and a numeric study. In the numeric study the performance of the different model formulations and the potentials of controlling unloading speeds are investigated with a set of custom instances.

As the problem belongs to the operational planning level and thus requires to be solved within a short time frame, a heuristic solution method is developed in the fifth chapter. A biased random-key genetic algorithm with a custom decoding scheme and an improvement procedure based on a Linear Program (LP) is introduced and explained. First, the specifics of the chosen representation are outlined and the evolutionary strategy is described. The LP-based improvement procedure can be applied to varying extend. Thus, distinct variants of the genetic algorithm that differentiate themselves through the application of the LP-based improvement procedure are outlined. The chapter ends with a numeric study to evaluate the performance of the three variants of the genetic algorithm for the instances considered in the previous chapter.

The sixth chapter investigates the practical applicability of truck schedules generated with the mathematical models using a discrete event simulation model. Observable uncertainties at parcel hubs are illustrated and the motivation to use simulation models in conjunction with mathematical models is outlined. The discrete event simulation model of the parcel hub allows the investigation of randomized unloading sequences and their impact on the applicability of optimized truck schedules. In order to apply optimized truck schedules generated using the mathematical models in the simulation model, three scheduling policies are developed that define the dispatching times of the trucks and the degree of flexibility in the unloading process. A simple first come first served rule is used as a reference. The scheduling policies are tested on the instance set of the previous chapters as part of a numeric study.

The seventh and final chapter summarizes the content and findings of the thesis and provides an outlook on further research potentials in the field of truck scheduling at parcel hubs.

2. Parcel handling in parcel hubs

2.1. Function and structural characteristics of parcel hubs

Parcel distribution in the postal service industry is mainly organized in less-than-truckload (LTT) freight networks. In LTT networks, carriers combine individual shipments that would not use the full capacity of a trailer by themselves[1] and weigh up to 10.000 lbs or about 4500 kg.[2] Since the allocated individual shipments usually do not share the same destination, LTT networks are frequently organized as hub-and-spoke networks where the carriers consolidate shipments at an intermediate stage of the network. For the postal service industry, service providers use parcel hubs as a redistribution point to consolidate parcel flows.[3] With the expansion of the parcel distribution industry, the number and size of parcel hubs has increased significantly.[4] In Germany, larger hubs such as the distribution center in Obertshausen operated by DHL process up to 50.000 parcels per hour.[5]

Parcel hubs are frequently organized according to the cross docking paradigm, where incoming freight moves through the distribution center with little or no intermediate time in storage and is directly loaded onto the outgoing trucks.[6] Compared to traditional distribution strategies, dwell times inside the distribution center and the needed storage space decreases and customer satisfaction increases due to shorter delivery times. Thus, cross docking is especially useful in distribution networks

---

[1] Jarrah et al. (2009, p. 611).
[2] V. F. Yu et al. (2008, p. 2).
[3] Boysen et al. (2017, p. 723).
[4] Morganti et al. (2014, p. 179).
[5] Tripp (2021, p. 394).
[6] Boysen and Fliedner (2010, p. 413).

for goods of a perishable nature, with high holding costs and in industries
where customers demand short delivery times - as it is the case for the
parcel service industry.[7]

2.2. Parcel hubs as a special type of cross docking hub

2.2.1. Usage of cross docking in supply chains

Parcel hubs are usually utilized in LTT distribution networks with cross
docking. The basic network structure in distribution networks with
cross docks usually consist of three stages: origins, cross docking hubs
and destinations.[8] A schematic view of a network with point-to-point
deliveries and a network with cross docking is given in Figure 2.1. In the
figure, circles represent origins and destinations, squares represent cross
docks.

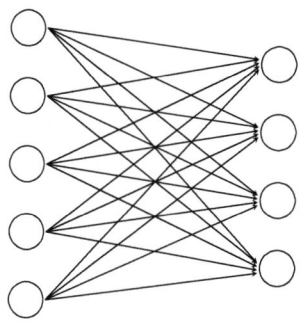
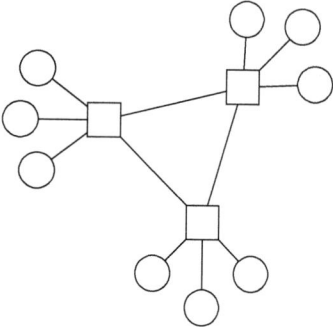

(a) Point-to-point network   (b) Cross docking network

Figure 2.1.: Network structures

In a point-to-point network, goods are often stored at the origins and sent
to their destinations once enough orders for a certain destination arrive.

---

[7]Van Belle et al. (2012, p. 829).
[8]Sung and Song (2003, p. 1283).

In some cases, goods are also stored in warehouses at the destinations. By contrast, in a distribution network with cross docking freight flows are processed on intermediate nodes of a hub-and-spoke network.[9] By consolidating shipments of different origins that share the same destination into full truck loads at cross docking hubs, economies of scale in transportation can be realized.[10] The benefits can be attributed to several factors. Firstly, vehicles in distribution networks with cross docking can use more efficient delivery routes since shipments are consolidated. Thus, transportation and labor costs are reduced. The consolidation also leads to a better utilization of the truck capacities and offers the opportunity to decrease the number of employed trucks or to use these trucks for different tasks. In the cross dock, the carrier usually sorts and ships the goods immediately after they arrive at the hub. Thus, little or no inventory is held at the distribution center and the order cycle time is reduced. This ensures a better match between the shipped quantities and the actual demand and improves the flexibility of the distribution network as a whole.[11] Thus, cross docking allows for a smooth flow of goods through the distribution network and is often utilized in the context of supply chains organized according to the just-in-time paradigm.[12]

The cross docking strategy needs the fulfilment of several prerequisites to fully utilize its benefits. Firstly, advanced information technology and suitable planning and management tools are essential to cope with extensive information flows. Further, the carrier has to actually consolidate shipments to full truck loads to exploit the benefits of completely utilized truck capacities. Closely connected, it is important to manage the physical flow of transported goods throughout the whole supply chain appropriately.[13] The efficient handling of freight flows within the cross dock hubs is crucial for the successful application of the strategy.

The prerequisites for successfully applying the cross docking strategy illustrated so far can be fulfilled by a proper design and management of the supply chain. However, several factors connected to the physical features of the transported goods and the characteristics of the market also determine whether the strategy can by applied successfully. Here, especially the demand rate and the stock-out costs of the goods are relevant as shown in Table 2.1. Cross docking generally leads to a lower

---

[9]Bányai et al. (2012, p. 84).
[10]Apte and Viswanathan (2000, p. 292).
[11]Apte and Viswanathan (2000, p. 297).
[12]Buijs et al. (2016, p. 213).
[13]Van Belle et al. (2012, p. 828).

Table 2.1.: Applicability of the cross docking concept (adapted from Apte and Viswanathan (2000))

		demand characteristics	
		stable	**unstable**
stock out costs	**high**	Cross docking possible (with proper tools and planning)	Traditional warehousing preferred
	low	Cross docking preferred	Cross docking possible (with proper tools and planning)

level of inventory and thus a higher probability of stock outs. When stock-out costs are high, cross docking is less appealing than for goods with low stock-out costs. Regarding demand, a stable demand rate leads to predictable transportation patterns and a greater degree of balance between the incoming and outgoing goods at the distribution center. Thus, the necessary measures and resources to synchronize the flow of goods through the distribution center can be managed more easily. If demand is unstable however, we observe greater fluctuations in the number of shipments arriving at and leaving the hub. Thus, the resulting lower degree of predictability renders managing the hub more difficult and requires further resources for dealing with an unsteady flow of goods.[14]

2.2.2. Consolidation of shipments in cross docking hubs

According to Van Belle et al. (2012) cross docking is "the process of unloading freight from inbound vehicles and loading these goods into outbound vehicles, with minimal handling and with little or no storage in between".[15] Consequentially, the layout and internal workflow in cross docks is designed to transfer goods through the hub with as little delay as possible. A schematic overview of freight handling at a cross dock hub is given in Figure 2.2.

The figure shows that inbound trucks contain parcels for a variety destinations whereas outbound trucks leave the hub containing parcels for a single destination only. We can divide the overall process of consolidating shipments in cross docks into three distinct phases:

---

[14]Apte and Viswanathan (2000, p. 297).
[15]Van Belle et al. (2012, p. 828).

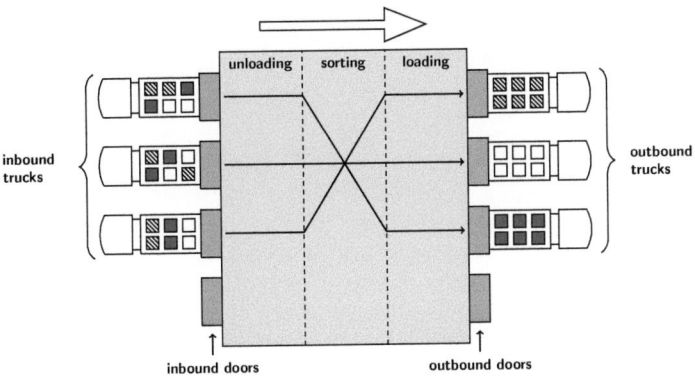

Figure 2.2.: Schematic layout of a cross docking terminal

(1) unloading shipments from inbound trucks at the inbound gates

(2) sorting and internal transport

(3) loading shipments onto outbound trucks at the outbound gates

When vehicles arrive at the cross dock, they usually first enter a parking space and wait to be assigned to an inbound door as part of the unloading process *(1)*. Once an inbound door and the necessary resources for unloading are available, the vehicle is dispatched to that gate and unloading starts. As a first step, the shipments are checked for potential damages and their destination is verified.[16]

For sorting and internal transport *(2)*, we differentiate between three basic concepts, namely *one-touch*, *single-stage* and *multi-stage* cross docking. When applying *one-touch* cross docking, commissioning, labeling etc. is performed on an earlier stage of the distribution network and the hub solely operates as a transfer terminal. Thus, incoming shipments are transferred to the outbound trucks directly. In contrast, in *one-stage* cross docking shipments are first staged in zones before being loaded to the outbound trucks. In *multi-stage* cross docks, workers recommission, label and repackage freight inside of the hub as part of the transfer process before they are loaded to the outbound trucks.[17] Therefore, some cross docks use designated temporary storage areas to perform those services.[18]

---

[16]W. Yu and Egbelu (2008, p. 378).
[17]Van Belle et al. (2012, p. 830) and Besse (2018, p. 14).
[18]Stephan and Boysen (2011, p. 130).

The storage areas also act as a buffer to synchronize the schedules of inbound and outbound trucks. In contrast to conventional warehouses, shipments usually only spend up to 24 hours in the storage areas of a cross dock.[19]

In most cases, incoming trucks contain shipments for several destinations that have to be sorted and transported to the designated outbound gates. Depending on the size and composition of the goods being consolidated at the cross dock, different means of internal transportation and sorting are employed. We distinguish between manual transportation with, e.g., forklifts, automated transportation systems with, e.g., conveyor belts and a combination of both. Manual transportation systems offer a greater degree of flexibility since they mainly employ human workers that are capable of reacting to variations in workloads. Further, expanding the workforce through overtime or temporary workers constitutes another option to react to workload peaks. In contrast, automated transportation systems have a fixed maximum capacity that cannot be exceeded and thus a tendency to be sensitive to workload variations. However, automated transportation systems also lead to a higher degree of efficiency for certain processes. In some cases, hub operators can use a combination of both transportation concepts with the result of both a higher degree of flexibility and increased efficiency at the same time.[20]

Once shipments arrive at the outbound doors, they are loaded onto the outbound trucks as part of the loading process (*3*). In most supply chains, outbound trucks wait until they are fully loaded before they depart from the cross dock. When shipments are rather small and of comparatively low value, however - as is is often the case, e.g., in LTT and parcel networks - trucks oftentimes leave the hub at predetermined fixed departure times and delayed shipments leave the hub later with a different vehicle.[21]

---

[19]Vis and Roodbergen (2008, pp. 677-678).
[20]Ladier and Alpan (2016a, p. 147).
[21]Boysen et al. (2013, p. 480).

2.3. Planning the design and operation of cross docking hubs

2.3.1. Planning problems at cross docking hubs

Planning problems at cross docking hubs are usually subdivided according to the planning horizon from long-term strategic over mid-term tactical to short-term operational problems. According to Stephan and Boysen (2011), the decision problems depicted in Table 2.2 are relevant in the context of designing and operating cross docks.

Table 2.2.: Relevant planning problems at cross docks

Time horizon	Planning problem	
Strategic	(i)	Location of the cross dock terminal
	(ii)	Layout of the terminal
Tactical	(iii)	Assignment of destinations to dock doors
Operational	(iv)	Truck scheduling
	(v)	Resource scheduling inside the hub

Since this dissertation mainly focuses on the operational planning problem of scheduling incoming trucks at parcel hubs, the adjacent planning problems shown in Table 2.2 are only illustrated briefly. An in-depth description of truck scheduling problems at cross docks follows in Chapter 3.

2.3.2. Strategic planning problems

Strategic planning problems at cross docks mainly concern long-term decisions on the design of the cross dock. The primary long term decisions are related to (i) the *location* and (ii) the *layout* of the cross dock.

(i) **Location of the cross dock terminal**
When deciding on the geographic location of a cross dock, the main influences stem from the overall network design[22] as well as other matters such as road access, legislation and social factors.[23] Out of these factors, a suitable location for a cross dock is especially dependent

---

[22]Mousavi and Vahdani (2016, p. 92).
[23]Ladier (2014, p. 9).

on the resulting freight flows throughout the network considering the already existing facilities.[24] The problem is in essence a facility location problem with specific additional features that are induced by the characteristics of cross docks such as the transshipment process at the hubs. Refer to Van Belle et al. (2012) for an overview of approaches for optimizing the location of cross docks.

(ii) **Layout of the cross dock terminal**
If the physical characteristics of a cross dock are not predetermined by external factors such as legal building regulations or the size and shape of the location the terminal is built on, decisions on the shape, size and number of doors of a cross dock have an influence on the performance of the hub.[25] In most cases, the goal is to have as many doors as possible. The physical shape of a cross dock can be described by a letter such as I, U, E, T, L, H or X.[26] According to Bartholdi and Gue (2004), the performance of a certain dock shape is best measured with the walking distances from door to door that result from a certain shape. They determine that for smaller hubs with less than about 150 doors the "I"-shape is suitable and should be expanded to a "T"-shape for medium size hubs. For large hubs with more than 200 doors they suggest an "X"-shape. However, Carlo and Bozer (2011) point out issues related to congestion and safety associated with the "X"-shape. Besides the shape of the terminal, the design of the internal storage areas or the means of transportation is also relevant with regard to the layout of the terminal. Vis and Roodbergen (2008) determine which locations should best be designated as storage areas inside the hub and Fedtke and Boysen (2017) investigate beneficial conveyor layouts for parcel hubs.

2.3.3. Tactical planning problems

Tactical planning problems have a shorter planning horizon (compared to strategic planning problems) of usually several months and the decisions are thus more easily reversible. With regard to tactical planning problems at cross docking hubs, decision makers mainly direct the general freight flows inside the hub by determining (iii) which destination is assigned to which outbound door.

---

[24]Buijs et al. (2014, p. 596).
[25]Vogt and Pienaar (2007, p. 94).
[26]Bartholdi and Gue (2004, p. 236).

(iii) **Assignment of destinations to dock doors**

The designation of doors as either inbound or outbound gates dictates the general direction of freight flows throughout the cross dock. Cross dock managers then have the opportunity of planning even more detailed freight flows by assigning origins and/or destinations to the fixed inbound and/or outbound doors.[27] The problem of assigning destinations to dock doors is frequently referred to as the Cross Dock Assignment Problem (CDAP). The overall objective is mostly to minimize the material handling costs of transferring the shipments through the cross dock. The door assignment is usually fixed for 3-6 month in case freight flows are relatively predictable and is referred to as *static* assignment. In some applications with more volatile freight flow patterns however, the assignment can also be conducted on a daily basis and is then called *dynamic* assignment. Naturally, frequent reassignment of doors enables greater potentials for optimization but requires further prerequisites with regard to the employed information technology and the flexibility of material handlers.[28]

For an overview of approaches for the CDAP, see Van Belle et al. (2012), Buijs et al. (2014) or Gelareh et al. (2020).

2.3.4. Operational planning problems

With a planning horizon usually ranging from less than a day to a week, operational planning problems at cross docks are primarily concerned with allocating the resources of the hub over the planning horizon to ensure an efficient flow of shipments through the hub. Here, especially (iv) scheduling incoming and/or outgoing trucks and (v) scheduling resources for transferring goods through the hub are important operational planning problems.[29]

(iv) **Truck Scheduling**

The main questions posed by the truck scheduling problem are *where* and *when* to process trucks at the gates of a cross dock. Here, the gates are seen as scarce resources. In this context, the term *where* refers to which gate the truck is assigned to and *when* to the time the truck is processed at the assigned gate. Truck schedules have a vital influence on the operational performance of the hub. For this reason,

---

[27] Agustina et al. (2010, p. 49).
[28] Buijs et al. (2014, p. 596).
[29] Agustina et al. (2010, p. 48).

the problem has been widely studied.[30] A detailed overview of truck scheduling problems at cross docks is given in Chapter 3.

The truck scheduling problem is often integrated into vehicle routing of the inbound and outbound trucks and was first investigated jointly by Y. H. Lee et al. (2006). For an overview of research on the combined problem setting, refer to Rotta et al. (2017).

(v) **Resource scheduling inside the hub**

Depending on the general organization of internal transport at the cross dock, different scheduling problems of the internal resources may arise. In all cases, the arriving shipments compete for scarce resources inside the hub such as temporary storage space, forklifts, conveyor belts or loading and unloading workers while travelling through the terminal.[31] An exemplary planning problem is scheduling workers for tasks such as breaking down incoming loads and assembling loads for outbound trucks as investigated by Li et al. (2004) or Alvarez-Perez et al. (2009). Planning transfer operations is also integrated into truck scheduling in some cases. With regard to integrated truck scheduling, Ladier and Alpan (2018) simultaneously schedule inbounds, outbounds and internal pallet handling operations. Integrated truck scheduling and workforce scheduling is investigated by Tadumadze et al. (2019) and Corsten et al. (2020). A more generalized look on the impact of internal resource requirements as a performance measurement is taken in Wolff et al. (2021).

2.4. Unique characteristics of parcel hubs in the context of cross docking

2.4.1. Impact of parcel transport characteristics on the design and operation of parcel hubs

As parcel hubs constitute a special form of cross dock, planning problems at parcel hubs are generally similar to those at other cross docks. However, the specifics of parcel transport influence the planning problems on different planning levels. Parcel service providers mainly transport smaller and relatively standardized shipments with limited weight, size

---

[30]Van Belle et al. (2012, p. 843).
[31]Stephan and Boysen (2011, p. 135).

and value. Further, customers of parcel service providers usually demand short delivery times. To achieve a high degree of cost efficiency and customer satisfaction, the industry transports large parcel volumes and employs methods such as standardization, process automation and parcel consolidation.[32]

Naturally, the mentioned distinctive characteristics of parcel transport dictate the structural design and operation of parcel hubs. Especially, the internal layout and organization of the hub is influenced by the specifics of parcel transport. While cross docking hubs in other industries often use forklifts or other manual means of transportation to transfer shipments from inbound doors to outbound doors, parcel hubs mainly operate with conveyor systems.[33] This can be attributed to the comparatively small size of the parcels and the large volumes of parcels that are processed at the hub. Further, parcel hubs rarely have any significant designated areas for longer-term storage due to a customer demand for short delivery times. Hence, deliveries leave the facility within 24 hours in the majority of cases.[34]

The general characteristics of parcel transport also influence parcel hubs at the tactical and operational level. Usually, the assignment of destinations to outbound gates is fixed over a midterm horizon since workers inside the hub often sort shipments according to their destinations manually. Thus, a more flexible assignment of outbound destinations would produce more errors in the manual sorting process. Inbound origins are however usually not fixed.[35] Due to the fixed assignment, the number of outbound doors is usually higher than the number of inbounds since outbound trucks wait for the arriving shipments at the outbound doors until they depart whereas inbounds are unloaded in a sequence at the inbound doors.

Since short delivery times are of high importance, oftentimes fixed departure schedules with strict deadlines are enforced for outbound trucks. Then, at the operational level the goal is to minimize the number of delayed shipments that would otherwise have to be transported the next day or with additional vehicles.[36]

---

[32]Clausen et al. (2015, p. 2).
[33]McWilliams et al. (2005, p. 394).
[34]Alpan et al. (2011, p. 385).
[35]Boysen et al. (2017, p. 725).
[36]Boysen et al. (2013, p. 480).

2.4.2. Internal transport with capacity constrained conveyors

As already established, the internal transport in parcel hubs is organized with conveyor networks in most cases. However, some parcels can potentially have specifications that prevent them from being transported on the conveyors such as extensive weight or an unwieldy geometry. Such irregular parcels are sorted and transported through the hub manually.[37] In the context of parcel hubs, the conveyor systems are organized either in *line* or *loop* configuration. The basic structure of line and loop conveyor systems is illustrated in Figure 2.3.

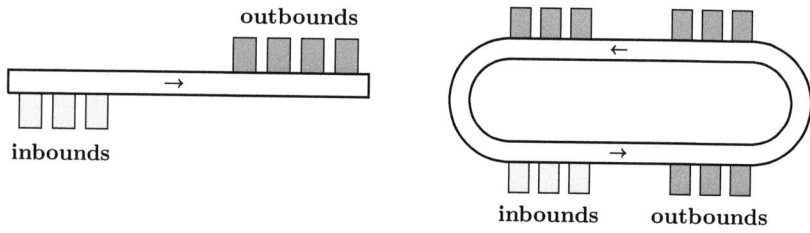

(a) Line conveyor configuration   (b) Loop conveyor configuration

Figure 2.3.: Schematic conveyor layouts at parcel hubs inspired by Haneyah et al. (2014)

In line configuration, parcels travel straight from the inbound doors to the outbound doors and remain in a designated area for unsorted parcels in case the outbound feeds are full. They then have to either be sorted manually or put on the conveyor again for a second time. In line configuration, a set of conveyors usually connects the inbound doors with a subset of outbound doors each. In loop configuration, only a single main conveyor is employed oftentimes. Further, unsorted parcels remain on the circular conveyor and pass the outbound feeds later on again. Thus, they do not have to be processed manually again but decrease the capacity of the conveyor system by remaining on the conveyor for an additional round.[38] Appropriately organized conveyor systems with a suitable assignment of destinations to outbounds provide the basis for an efficient transfer of parcels through the hub. However, the capacity of the conveyor system is limited. Especially inbound truck scheduling has

---

[37]Clausen et al. (2015, p. 1925).
[38]Haneyah et al. (2014, p. 148).

a critical impact on the actual parcel flows on the conveyors and can lead to congestion if too many trucks with parcels designated for the same conveyors are scheduled at the same time. In such a case, congestion is often managed reactively by stopping or slowing the unloading process of those trucks that contribute to the congestion the most.[39] In the postal service industry, the content and loading pattern of the individual trucks is mostly only roughly known and the parcels leave the trucks in a mostly arbitrary sequence.[40] Thus, determining the impact of a specific truck schedule on congestion inside the hub cannot be determined with certainty and thus only be estimated. To use the conveyor capacity effectively, the trucks first have to be scheduled according to the information available to the scheduler. However, the resulting flows might still lead to congestion due to the lack of precise information on the exact parcel composition in the trucks and the resulting unloading sequences. The managers responsible for the parcel flow then have the option to fine-tune the parcel flows by influencing the unloading speed of individual inbound trucks by reassigning workers to avoid congestion on the conveyors.

2.4.3. Significance of deadlines and fixed outbound departure schedules

Shipments in the postal service industry are mostly small and have comparatively low value. Therefore, the parcel composition and arrangement inside each inbound truck may only be roughly known and may only become apparent once the trailer is opened at the parcel hub.[41] Letting outbound trucks wait for each shipment dedicated for them until the truck is fully loaded would frequently lead to delays for all shipments with the same destination. As customers demand short delivery times and interconnected delivery services such as next day deliveries become increasingly more popular,[42] hub operators aim to avoid such delays and thus apply fixed outbound schedules where each outbound truck receives a fixed departure time at which it leaves the terminal even if it is not fully loaded. A fixed departure schedule ensures that a majority of parcels depart without delay and leads to a steady flow of trucks and parcels in the distribution network.[43] A steady flow of parcels is

---

[39]McWilliams et al. (2005, p. 396).
[40]Boysen et al. (2013, p. 480).
[41]Boysen et al. (2013, p. 480).
[42]Morganti et al. (2014, p. 188).
[43]Boysen et al. (2013, p. 480).

especially important in larger hub-and-spoke networks where shipments pass through several stages, i.e, form one cross dock to the next. Here, delays can have significant consequences on the performance of the whole network.[44]

Parcels that did not arrive before the deadline remain at the hub and have to either be temporarily stored and shipped at a later point in time or redirected to costly additional vehicles specially assigned to delivering tardy shipments. Thus, an efficient handling of shipments at the parcel hub is crucial to avoid additional costs due to additional vehicles, double-handling or related to decreased customer satisfaction through delayed shipments. In this context, optimized inbound truck schedules constitute a promising approach to avoid delays.[45]

---

[44]Ishfaq and Sox (2012, p. 629).
[45]Boysen and Fliedner (2010, p. 413).

3. Inbound truck scheduling at parcel hubs

3.1. Classification of truck scheduling problems at cross docking hubs

3.1.1. Classification framework

The truck scheduling problem at cross docking hubs has already been widely studied due to the significance of inbound truck schedules for the operational performance of cross docks themselves and the distribution network as a whole. Since cross docks are utilized for a variety of distribution networks and applications, a classification scheme for specific truck scheduling problems has already been established by Boysen and Fliedner (2010). The descriptions of truck scheduling problems of this section follow their classification scheme. Before illustrating the characteristics of truck scheduling problems at parcel hubs, a general overview of truck scheduling problems at cross docks is given.

The truck scheduling problem at cross docks has a close relation to traditional machine scheduling and can be interpreted as a two stage parallel machine scheduling problem, where trucks constitute jobs and inbound and outbound gates reflect machines.[1] Thus, the classification scheme for truck scheduling at cross docks is mainly inspired by the three field notation for scheduling problems by Graham et al. (1979). The so called *Graham*-notation classifies scheduling problems according to the machine environment (α), job characteristics (β) and objective function (γ). When applied to the truck scheduling problem at cross docks, α refers to the gate characteristics, β to the operational characteristics and γ again to the objective. The tupel $[\alpha \mid \beta \mid \gamma]$ specifies individual problems. In the following, common problem settings for truck scheduling at cross docks are illustrated following the classification scheme and description

---

[1] Boysen and Fliedner (2010, p. 415).

of Boysen and Fliedner (2010) with the assumption of a deterministic planning setting. For extensive literature reviews of the field of cross dock scheduling refer to Boysen and Fliedner (2010), Van Belle et al. (2012), Ladier and Alpan (2016a) and Theophilus et al. (2019).

3.1.2. Gate characteristics

With regard to the gate characteristics α of truck scheduling problems at cross docks, the categorization addresses the service mode (α_1) and number of available gates (α_2).

The service mode specifies the degree of flexibility in the gate usage. Settings with the lowest degree of flexibility correspond to $\alpha_1 = E$ where gates are explicitly used as either inbound gates or outbound gates and is the most frequently assumed service mode setting. If gates are used in mixed service mode, inbound and outbound trucks can use all available gates ($\alpha_1 = M$). In some cases a combination of both service modes can be observed and thus some gates are used explicitly for inbounds or outbounds whereas other operate in mixed service mode ($\alpha_1 = EM$). Lastly, $\alpha_1 = G$ refers to settings where each individual truck is assigned to a specific gate. The problem can then rather be designated as sequencing problem. Thus, we determine a sequence of the assigned trucks for each gate.[2]

A comparative study of combined inbound and outbound truck scheduling with gate usage in exclusive or mixed mode can be found in Berghman et al. (2015). Rijal et al. (2019) investigate the potentials of using gates in mixed service mode when combining the dock door assignment problem with the truck scheduling problem. Further, Bodnar et al. (2017) consider a cross dock with mixed service gates and temporary storage with the focus on minimizing the tardiness of shipments. Shahmardan and Sajadieh (2020) examine a problem setting where trucks can be partially unloaded and are potentially used as both inbound or outbound trucks and thus naturally consider gates in mixed service mode.

The number of available gates can either be arbitrary or fixed to a certain number k ($\alpha_2 = k$). The number of gates is usually fixed to determine the complexity for a problem setting or to estimate a limit to the objective function value. For example, by setting the number of gates to one, an upper or lower limit for an application with a multitude of gates can be generated. The number of gates is mostly arbitrary

---

[2]Boysen and Fliedner (2010, p. 416).

when reflecting most practical applications. When approaching the truck scheduling problem as a classical scheduling problem, many studies only consider a single inbound and a single outbound gate. Examples for this approach are W. Yu and Egbelu (2008) who investigate a cross dock with limited storage capacities and Arabani et al. (2012) who include multiple objective functions for the problem setting. Further, F. Chen and C.-Y. Lee (2009) use a two-machine flowshop formulation for the truck scheduling problem where operations on the first machine represent the unloading process at the inbound gates and operations on the second machine represent the loading process at the outbound gates. Boysen et al. (2010) reformulate the problem with a time horizon split into time intervals. Generally, once the problem setting allows an aggregated view of inbound and outbound gates rather than dictating that trucks have to be assigned to a specific gate, the problem can be reduced to the one inbound and one outbound door case. For further reference, Ladier and Alpan (2016a) provide an extensive overview of cross dock truck scheduling research and classify studies with regard to the number of inbound and outbound gates.

3.1.3. Operational characteristics

The operational characteristics encompass all structural restrictions and particularities of a specific problem setting that influence the scheduling of trucks and handling of shipments inside the hub. Boysen and Fliedner (2010) distinguish between nine categories of characteristics as summarized in Table 3.1.

β_1 **Preemption**
When preemption is allowed ($\beta_1 = prmt$), trucks docked to inbound or outbound gates may leave the gate and continue unloading at a later point in time. Most practical applications do not consider preemption.[3] However, the theoretical optimization potentials of preempting the unloading process has been addressed in Mohtashami (2015) who compares the resulting makespan of the overall unloading and transshipment process for a scenario with fixed holding patterns of outbound trucks and a scenario where preemption is allowed. Ye et al. (2018) investigate the problem with additional constraints regarding fixed loading and unloading sequences.

---

[3] Ladier and Alpan (2016a, p. 147).

Table 3.1.: Specific operational truck scheduling characteristics at cross docks

β	Operational characteristic
β_1	preemption
β_2	arrival times
β_3	processing time
β_4	deadlines
β_5	intermediate storage
β_6	assignment restrictions
β_7	transshipment time
β_8	outbound organization
β_9	interchangeable products

β_2 Arrival times

Trucks can either arrive throughout the planning horizon at arrival time at_j ($\beta_2 = at_j$) or are already available from the start and thus have no restrictions to the earliest possible starting time for unloading. Arrival times distributed over the planning horizon and concentrated arrivals at the beginning can be found almost equally in the literature and are usually not the focus of investigation.[4]

β_3 Processing time

The processing time p_j includes the time needed for all activities that are associated with the unloading process for inbound trucks and the loading process for outbound trucks. For the scope of this overview, deterministic processing times are assumed. The processing time can vary for different trucks in case of a heterogeneous fleet and/or quantity shipments per truck. In industries with shipments of comparative size and comparable vehicle capacities and in case of homogeneous average truck loads, the assumption of identical processing times might also be valid ($\beta_3 = (p_j = p)$).[5] As an example, McWilliams and McBride (2013) use the assumption of identical processing times when formalizing the problem by dividing the planning horizon into periods according to the processing time of the trucks. In some applications, processing times are similar but varied, and are thus taken from a specified interval of processing times ($\beta_3 = (\underline{p} \leq p_j \leq \overline{p})$).

---

[4]Ladier and Alpan (2016a, p. 146).
[5]Boysen and Fliedner (2010, p. 417).

β_4 Deadlines

In many practical problem settings deadlines or due dates $\overline{d}_\lambda$ are imposed on inbound and/or outbound trucks and thus define the time these trucks have to leave the cross dock. The classification scheme by Boysen and Fliedner (2010) specifies subscripts for $\beta_4 = \lambda$ to define which trucks or shipments are subjected to deadlines:

$\lambda = i$: Inbounds are subjected to deadlines or due dates.

$\lambda = o$: Outbounds are subjected to deadlines or due dates.

$\lambda = j$: Inbounds and outbounds are subjected to deadlines or due dates.

$\lambda = s$: Individual shipments are subjected to specific due dates or deadlines.

Ladier and Alpan (2016a) state that in nearly all practical reference cases deadlines are imposed on both inbound and outbound trucks but only about half of all research studies they found in their review reference deadlines. Thus, they point out a gap between current research and the practical implementation of cross docking. Deadlines are most relevant when cross docks handle deliveries as service providers for customers as violating deadlines would lead to decreased customer satisfaction. For cross docks that are part of a company's own supply chain deadlines are often agreed upon and the consequences of not meeting a deadline are mostly less severe.[6]

β_5 Intermediate storage

Depending on the characteristics of the transported goods, cross docks usually have designated areas for short-term storage where shipments remain until they are processed further and loaded to the outbound trucks.[7] These areas can either be assumed to be *unlimited* in case they are irrelevant with regard to the transshipment process or *limited* if they are seen as a scarce resource. In supply chains with refrigerated goods for example, the intermediate storage area is often assumed to be *zero* ($\beta_5 = no - wait$) since goods have to be proceed immediately without delay to outbound trucks to not break the cold chain in a non-chilled facility.

A majority of studies do not consider limited storage capacities inside

---

[6]Ladier and Alpan (2016a, p. 146).
[7]Van Belle et al. (2012, p. 832).

the hub.[8] Boysen (2010) addresses the special case of truck scheduling at cross docks without any storage in the context of an application in a food supply chain. Further, Joo and Kim (2013) consider a specific supply chain with so called compound trucks that are used as both inbound and outbound trucks and thus have to immediately be loaded after being unloaded. In a similar regard, Golias et al. (2013) study a cross dock where shipments are transported directly using forklifts from inbound trucks to outbound trucks according to requests without being stored in between.

β_6 **Assignment restrictions**

Restrictions concerning the doors a truck can be assigned to apply in case the truck exhibits characteristics with regard to its size or load that would confine it to a subset of the available doors ($\beta_6 = doors$). Such characteristics include the size of the cargo, cooling requirements or special material handling equipment. If a trucks shipments are relatively homogeneous with regard to their size, weight, geometry etc. and do not require additional measures to be unloaded, the truck can usually be assigned to every door without restrictions.[9]

β_7 **Transshipment time**

The transshipment time refers to the time it takes for a shipment to reach a certain outbound gate once unloaded at a specific inbound gate. This time span depends on several factors that are specific to the problem setting, for example the relative position of the inbound and outbound gate, the availability and operational speed of transfer resources or congestion inside the hub.[10]

In case individual transshipment times between specific inbound and outbound doors are included ($\beta_7 = t_{io}$), the assignment of inbound and outbound trucks to specific doors influences the operational performance of the hub. Here, we usually assume that transporting shipments between doors that are closer together also leads to shorter transshipment times. When assuming specific transshipment times, reducing the problem to a 1-inbound and 1-outbound problem is not possible.[11] Assuming door specific transshipment times reflects the circumstances at real world terminals the closest.

When transshipment times do not vary significantly for all inbound

---

[8]Theophilus et al. (2019).
[9]Boysen and Fliedner (2010, p. 417).
[10]Maknoon et al. (2017, p. 169).
[11]Ladier and Alpan (2016a, p. 150).

trucks, a common simplification of the real world setting is to assume
constant transshipment times. With constant transshipment times
the complexity of the problem is greatly reduced and a 1-inbound and
1-outbound formulation is applicable. A further simplification would
be to completely neglect transshipment times ($\beta_7 = (t_j = 0)$) which
is relevant to identify structural properties of the problem setting or
when transshipment times are negligible compared to the unloading
and/or loading times.[12]

β_8 **Outbound organization**
Outbound trucks can either leave the hub as soon as they are fully
loaded or at a predefined fixed point in time independent of their
loading status ($\beta_8 = fix$). Especially in multi-stage distribution
networks fixed outbound departures find frequent usage as illustrated
in Section 2.4.3 on page 17.

β_9 **Interchangeable products**
Shipments processed a the hub can either be unique and thus dedicated to a specific outbound truck or belong to a specified category of
products that can be loaded to any outbound truck with a demand for
the category of products interchangeably ($\beta_9 = change$). Interchangeability allows for a greater degree of flexibility but is not applicable
if products cannot actually be used interchangeably.[13] An example
is the postal service industry where each shipment is dedicated for
specific receivers.
Similarly, Tootkaleh et al. (2016) investigate interchangeability in a
setting with fixed outbound plans. Further, research on interchangeability can be found in Serrano et al. (2017) who consider a specific
problem setting in the automotive industry.

3.1.4. Objectives

Some potential objective functions for truck scheduling problems at
cross docks are conceptually identical to those employed for traditional
machine scheduling problems whereas others are directly connected to
the particularities of the problem setting of cross docks. Boysen and
Fliedner (2010) illustrate the following objective functions.
An example for a traditional objective function is the minimization

---

[12]Boysen and Fliedner (2010, p. 417).
[13]Tootkaleh et al. (2016, p. 52).

of the **makespan or schedule length** ($\gamma = C_{max}$) which is used in academic works on the problem most frequently.[14] Here, the goal is to minimize the total time to process all inbound and outbound trucks. The schedule length is often described as having a significant impact on the operational costs.[15] With specific regard to the truck scheduling problem, the minimization of the **weighted sum of completion times** ($\gamma = \sum_\lambda w_\lambda C_\lambda$) where λ can refer to specific shipments $s \in S$ or outbound trucks $o \in \mathcal{O}$ is a suitable objective when the goal is to ensure that specific trucks leave the hub as soon as possible. C_λ refers to the completion time and w_λ is the weight of a shipment or truck. With appropriate values for w_λ, important shipments and/or outbound trucks can receive a priority status and thus tend to be processed earlier.

In operational settings where deadlines are relevant, aiming to minimize the **maximum lateness** L_{max} for all shipments s or outbound trucks o ($\gamma = L_{max}$) is an option. The maximum lateness for shipments is defined as the maximum time difference between the deadline and the actual completion time of all shipments, formally $L_{max} = \max_{s \in S}[C_s - d_s]$ where d_s refers to the deadline of shipment s. Applying maximum lateness leads to schedules that tend to allow a number of smaller delays but prevents outliers of bigger delays.[16] Lateness evaluates the deviation of a jobs completion time from its deadline. In a resulting optimized schedule, jobs are planned as far from the deadline as possible. Another similar optimization criterion referencing deadlines is the **minimization of tardiness** which is formally defined as $T_s = \max[0, C_s - d_s]$. Here, every job completed before its deadline receives the same value of zero.[17] In case even small delays of selected shipments or outbound trucks are deemed more significant, minimizing the weighted sum of the tardiness of all shipments ($\gamma = \sum_\lambda w_\lambda T_\lambda$) is reasonable.[18] However, in some applications the extend of the delays is irrelevant and even small delays have detrimental effects. Then, the objective is to minimize the weighted number of tardy shipments or trucks $\sum_\lambda w_\lambda U_\lambda$, where $U_\lambda = 1$, if $C_\lambda > d_\lambda$ ($\gamma = \sum_\lambda w_\lambda U_\lambda$).[19]

Minimizing the usage of **intermediate storage space** of the hub can also be an objective with regard to the truck scheduling problem. A

---

[14]Ladier and Alpan (2016a, p. 153).
[15]McWilliams et al. (2005, p. 393)
[16]Malve and Uzsoy (2007, p. 3017).
[17]Erickson et al. (2014, p. 7).
[18]Vepsalainen and Morton (1987, p. 1035).
[19]Boysen and Fliedner (2010, p. 418).

decreased inventory level often leads to less congestion inside the hub and faster processing of shipments. Therefore, storing shipments is disincentivized. One approach is to minimize the total number of stored shipments for each product category ($\gamma = \sum_p w_p S_\lambda$). An alternative approach is to **minimize the maximum inventory level** ($\gamma = S_{max}$). For some settings, simply finding a feasible solution for a given instance and thus **refraining from stating an objective function** ($\gamma = -$) is a valid approach, for example when testing whether deadlines can be met at all. Note that combining objectives in a multi-objective approach is also possible.

3.2. Truck scheduling at parcel hubs

As already established, parcel hubs are a special version of cross docks. Thus, the truck scheduling problem at parcel hubs constitutes a special case of the truck scheduling problem at cross docking hubs. With reference to the illustrated particularities of parcel hubs in Section 2.4, the truck scheduling problem at parcel hubs has unique characteristics with regard to the outbound organization, usage of capacity constrained conveyors for internal transport and the properties of parcel shipment.

Regarding outbound organization, parcel hubs mostly use fixed outbound plans. Fixed departure times are also relevant when considering multimodal cross docks of, e.g., the air cargo industry when strict flight plans have to be followed as investigated by Ou et al. (2010). Fixed outbound plans have also been researched more generally by Molavi et al. (2018) who integrate inbound and outbound truck scheduling with fixed departure plans and Tootkaleh et al. (2016) who consider fixed departure plans in a cross dock with product substitution and minimize the inventory holding costs. With regard to the postal service industry, Boysen et al. (2013) consider the problem setting under the assumption that each outbound gate is only occupied by a single truck. Contrary to the approaches mentioned before, the number of tardy shipments constitutes the optimization criterion whereas the other approaches only consider deadlines with regard to the feasibility of truck schedules.

Another field of research on truck scheduling in the postal service industry focuses on the efficient usage of conveyors inside the hub. McWilliams et al. (2005) were the first to study the operational scheduling of trucks at parcel hubs minimizing the makespan and focus on avoiding congestion inside the hub with a simulation-based approach. A similar simulation-based approach by Clausen et al. (2017) also focuses on minimizing congestion by minimizing the maximum conveyor usage. Further, McWilliams et al. (2008) illustrate the problem when assuming trailers with unequal sizes. McWilliams and McBride (2013) present further adjacent research on the approximation of transfer times, McWilliams (2009a) and Haneyah et al. (2014) investigate load-balancing on conveyors in parcel hubs. In a more generalized setting of hubs used in LTT-networks, Maknoon et al. (2016) explore scheduling strategies to efficiently use the transshipment resources. Serrano et al. (2017) also consider transshipment resources for cross docks in the automotive industry and explicitly model repackaging operations inside the facility.

Some parcel hubs utilize conveyors in loop configuration as illustrated in Section 2.4.2. Boysen et al. (2017) investigate the truck scheduling problem on cyclic conveyors under the assumption of fixed deadlines and aim to minimize the distances parcels have to travel on the conveyors. Zenker and Boysen (2017) also consider truck scheduling with conveyors in loop configuration but focus on an application where dock sharing of inbound and outbound trucks is allowed. Further, for applications where cyclic conveyors with short cuts are present, J. C. Chen et al. (2019) integrate the opportunities of alternative parcel routing into the problem setting. Table 3.2 summarizes the relevant literature.

Table 3.2.: Literature overview of relevant truck scheduling problems

author	minimize tardy shipments	fixed departure plans	capacitated transfer resources	conveyors	postal service industry
Ou et al. (2010)		x			
Tootkaleh et al. (2016)		x			
Maknoon et al. (2016)			x		
Serrano et al. (2017)			x		
McWilliams et al. (2005)			x	x	x
McWilliams et al. (2008)			x	x	x
McWilliams and McBride (2013)			x	x	x
Clausen et al. (2017)			(x)	x	x
Boysen et al. (2013)	x	x			x
Molavi et al. (2018)		x		x	x
Boysen et al. (2017)		x		x	x
J. C. Chen et al. (2019)		x		x	x
Zenker and Boysen (2017)		x		x	x

To conclude, research on scheduling trucks in parcel hubs mostly either focuses on throughput maximization on specific types of conveyors or minimizing parcel delays in the context of fixed outbound organization. Thus, the remainder of this work is dedicated to closing the literature gap by considering both limited conveyor capacity and fixed deadlines in conjunction for the parcel hub scheduling problem and including the particularities of the postal service industry. Further, approaches to incorporate flexibility in the unloading process are investigated.

4. Model formulations for the Parcel Hub Scheduling Problem with Limited Conveyor Capacities (PHSP-LCC)

4.1. Basic problem statement for the PHSP-LCC

The following chapter is dedicated to illustrating several mathematical formulations for the truck scheduling problem at parcel hubs. As established in Chapter 3, the distinctive features of the problem setting include limited conveyor capacities, fixed outbound departures and the particularities of parcel transport. The referenced hub uses conveyors in line configuration. The model is not directly applicable to hubs with loop configuration. The PHSP-LCC has already been outlined in Bugow and Kellenbrink (2023).

Irrespective of the particular modeling approach, the following basic assumptions are considered.

(i) The parcel hub possesses a specific number of inbound and outbound doors in exclusive service mode.

(ii) Inbound and outbound doors are connected via a system of conveyor belts. Parcels unloaded at the inbound doors can reach every outbound door irrespective of the specific inbound gate they are unloaded at. Each conveyor serves a subset of all outbound doors.

(iii) Conveyor capacities are limited.

(iv) Outbound trucks are already present at the beginning of the planning horizon.

(v) Each outbound truck is assigned to a specific outbound door. Further, only a single outbound truck is processed at each outbound door. Therefore, the outbound trucks do not have to be scheduled.

(vi) Outbound trucks leave the hub at a predefined deadline irrespective of the number of loaded parcels. All parcels that arrive late are considered tardy and have to be stored or processed otherwise. Additional handling steps for tardy parcels are not considered in the model.

(vii) Transshipment times inside the hub are small compared to inbound truck unloading times and do not vary significantly for different destinations. Thus, they are neglected.

(viii) Inbound trucks arrive throughout the planning horizon and can potentially be processed at every inbound door. The number of loaded parcels and their respective destination is known.

(ix) Once an inbound truck starts the unloading process, it can only leave the door again after all parcels have been unloaded from the truck. Thus, preemption is not allowed.

(x) It is irrelevant to which inbound door arriving inbound trucks are assigned to since transshipment times are neglected, all inbound doors are available to all inbound trucks and each inbound door is connected to every outbound doors via the conveyors.

In general, the goal is to find a truck schedule that states the starting times of all inbound trucks. The central decision is *when* to start the unloading process of *which* inbound truck. It has to ensure that the number of concurrently unloaded inbound trucks does not exceed the number of available doors and the number of concurrently transferred parcels on each conveyor does not exceed its capacity. The goal is to maximize the number of parcels arriving on time.

Two basic modelling approaches are followed in this thesis: *time-indexed* or *interval-based*. In a *time-indexed* approach the planning horizon is divided into discrete time periods[1] which allows us to model the decision in which period an inbound truck starts unloading. Further, we can model the utilization of conveyors and doors in each period. Similarly, an *interval-based* approach defines a number of time intervals that encompass

---

[1]Van den Akker et al. (2000, p. 111).

parts of the planning horizon.[2] The model is then based on the decision
in which interval an inbound truck is processed. Further, by defining
which intervals overlap we can also model the resulting conveyor and
door utilization. Figure 4.1 illustrates the idea of both a time-indexed
and an interval-based approach by indicating the unloading process with
a length of four time units of an inbound truck starting at the beginning
of period $t = 1$ and $t = 2$.

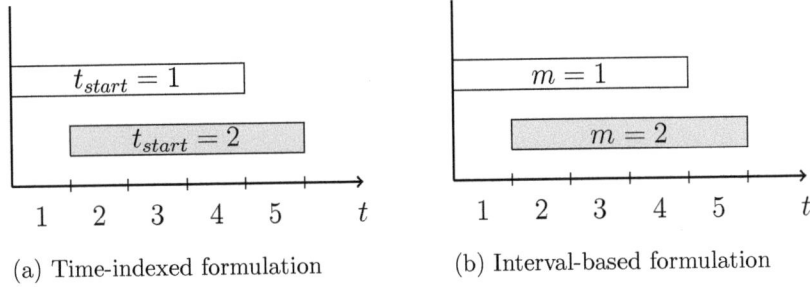

(a) Time-indexed formulation   (b) Interval-based formulation

Figure 4.1.: Time-indexed and interval-based modeling approaches

Another alternative approach is a *sequence-based* formulation that indicates precedence relations between individual inbound trucks. However,
the inbound doors are not considered as separate entities in the problem
setting. Thus, the formulation would have to include additional restrictions that determine the concurrently processed inbound trucks and
information on *which* gate an inbound truck is assigned to. Consequentially, the advantage of the interval-based and time-indexed approaches
of only having to specify *when* an inbound truck is processed diminishes.
Further difficulties would arise when formulating the capacity constraints
since only the relation of individual trucks with each other is defined
and not *when* they are processed. Due to the stated disadvantages of a
sequence-based formulation, the remainder of the thesis only addresses
time-indexed and interval-based formulations of the problem.
To generally illustrate the impact of the inbound truck schedule on the
workload, consider the following exemplary setting of a hub with four
inbound trucks and two outbound trucks. Table 4.1 shows the parameters
of the inbound and outbound trucks.

---

[2]Kolen et al. (2007, p. 531).

Table 4.1.: Inbound truck parameters of the example

		parcels for outbounds	
inbound	unloading speed	$o1$	$o2$
$i1$	10	100	0
$i2$	10	70	30
$i3$	10	10	90
$i4$	10	50	50

Unloading speed in parcels per minute.

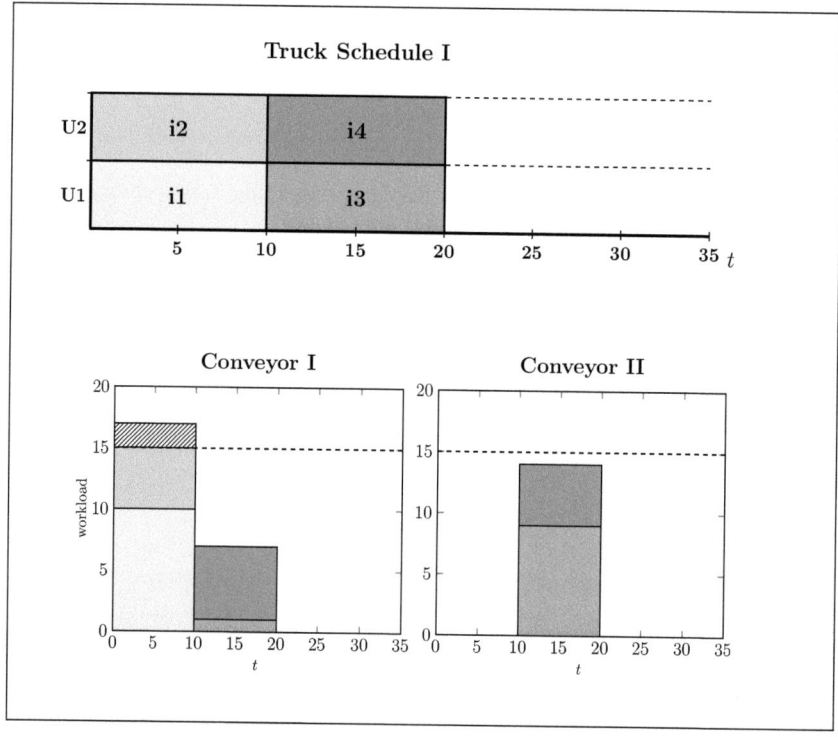

Figure 4.2.: First exemplary truck schedule

Each inbound truck includes shipments for at least one of the two out-bound trucks and is unloaded with a fixed unloading speed. Inbound

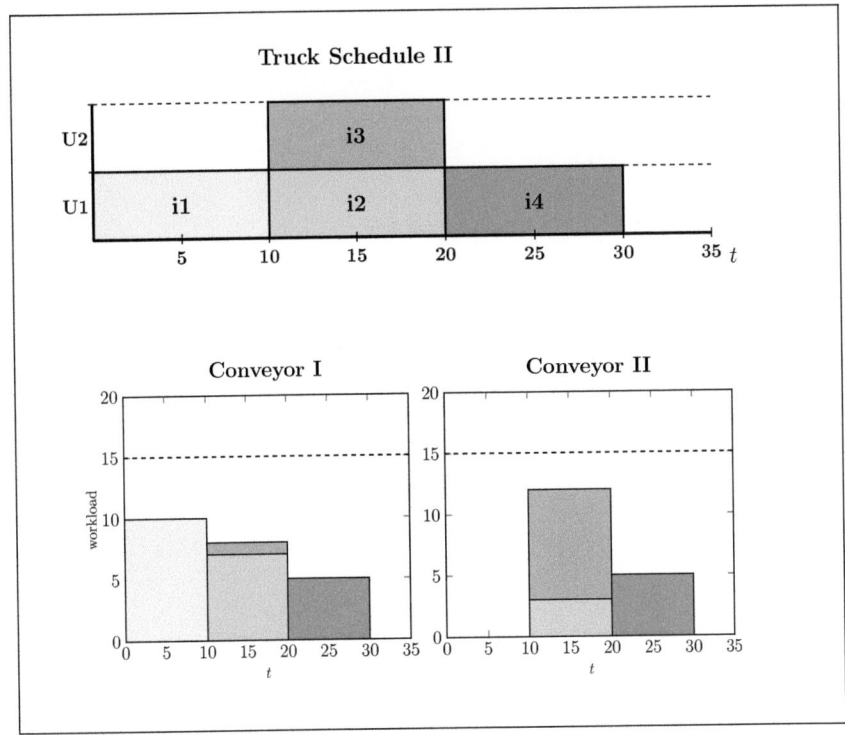

Figure 4.3.: Second exemplary truck schedule

trucks can be unloaded at two distinct inbound doors $U1$ and $U2$. Since each outbound truck is only assigned to a specific outbound gate, the outbound gates $O1$ and $O2$ as well as outbound trucks $o1$ and $o2$ do not have to be differentiated. Shipments reach the outbound gates via two conveyors that are only connected to one of the two outbound gates. Conveyor I is connected to $O1$, Conveyor II to $O2$. The conveyors both have a capacity of 15 parcels per minute, respectively. Based on this information, a first approach to generate a truck schedule that does not consider the conveyor capacities would be to first assign the trucks $i1$ to $U1$ and $i2$ to $U2$ followed by $i3$ and $i4$. The resulting schedule and conveyor utilization is shown in Figure 4.2 and Truck Schedule I.

We can observe that all trucks could potentially be unloaded within 20 minutes with this approach. However, the capacity on the first conveyor

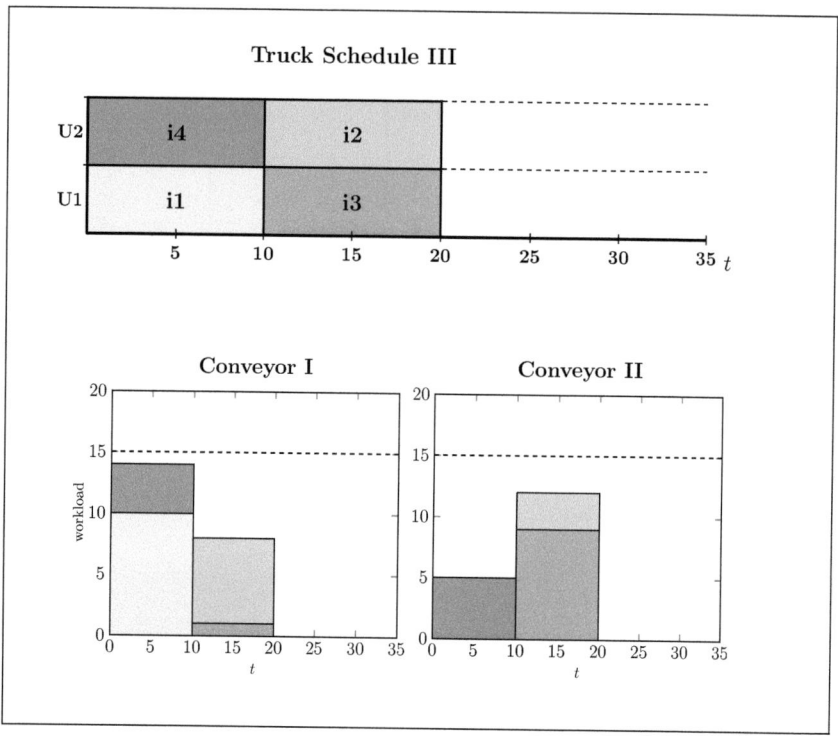

Figure 4.4.: Third exemplary truck schedule

would be exceeded and thus delays through congestion would follow. To avoid congestion on the first conveyor, truck $i2$ could be unloaded after the unloading process of $i1$ is finished as shown in Truck Schedule II in Figure 4.3.

In this case, the capacity of the first conveyor would not be exceeded but the last inbound truck $i4$ would finish unloading significantly later resulting in a schedule length of 30 minutes. By altering the sequence, we can however decrease the total length of the schedule without overburdening the conveyors as shown in Truck Schedule III in Figure 4.4.

The third schedule considers the impact individual inbound trucks have on the conveyor utilization at schedules inbound $i1$ and $i4$ as well as $i2$ and $i3$ concurrently to avoid congestion. Thus, the capacity on the conveyors is not exceeded and the schedule length is reduced. The example illustrates how explicitly including scarce conveyor capacities in scheduling decisions of the inbound trucks is crucial to the performance of the parcel hub.

In the following, first mathematical models assuming fixed unloading speeds are presented. Based on these models, formulations for the problem setting allowing controllable unloading speeds are introduced.

4.2. Model formulations for the PHSP-LCC-fix

4.2.1. The time-indexed PHSP-LCC-fix

Assumptions and notation

The following section presents the assumptions and notation for the time-indexed formulation of the **P**arcel **H**ub **S**cheduling **P**roblem with **L**imited **C**onveyor **C**apacity and **Fix**ed Unloading Speeds (PHSP-LCC-fix).

According to the time-indexed modelling approach, discrete time periods $t \in \mathcal{T}$ with $\mathcal{T} = \{1, \ldots, T\}$ are used. An inbound truck $i \in \mathcal{I}$ with $\mathcal{I} = \{1, \ldots, I\}$ arrives at the start of period at_i. Therefore, inbound truck i can be unloaded in periods $t \in \mathcal{T}_i$ with $\mathcal{T}_i = \{at_i, \ldots, T\}$. As the unloading speed is fixed, the inbound truck requires a fixed unloading time d_i.

The cross dock has U inbound doors. The decision on which specific door an inbound is assigned to is irrelevant. Thus, the doors are not modelled separately as it makes no difference which inbound door is selected for unloading with regard to the duration of the overall process.

Since each outbound truck $o \in \mathcal{O}$ with $\mathcal{O} = \{1, \ldots, O\}$ is uniquely assigned to one outbound door, there is no distinction between outbound doors and outbound trucks. A number of $ship_{io}$ parcels from inbound truck i is designated for outbound truck o.

Conveyor $k \in \mathcal{K}$ with $\mathcal{K} = \{1, \ldots, K\}$ has a capacity of r_k parcels per period. Regarding the basic assumptions, each inbound door can access each conveyor. In contrast, each outbound door is assigned to only one conveyor. The subset $\mathcal{O}_k$ contains all outbound doors that are connected to conveyor k.

Parcels for the different conveyors are assumed to be homogeneously or evenly distributed in the truck. The unloading rate lr_{ik} of parcels from inbound truck i for conveyor k per period is therefore defined as follows:

$$lr_{ik} = \frac{\sum_{o \in \mathcal{O}_k} ship_{io}}{d_i} \tag{4.1}$$

The objective function of the model aims to maximize the number of parcels arriving on time. A deadline in period dl_o represents an outbound truck o leaving at the end of this period, meaning that it can be loaded until period dl_o. The parameter uf_{ito} indicates the number of parcels arriving on time for outbound truck o if inbound truck i is scheduled to start in period t. It is defined by the following equation:

$$uf_{ito} = \begin{cases} ship_{io}, & t \leq dl_o - d_i \\ \frac{dl_o - t + 1}{d_i} \cdot ship_{io}, & dl_o - d_i < t \leq dl_o \\ 0, & t > dl_o \end{cases} \tag{4.2}$$

Consider an example illustrated in Figure 4.5. The unloading time d_i of truck $i1, i2$ and $i3$ equals 10 periods. For inbound truck $i1$, the unloading process is scheduled to start in period $t1$ and all of the parcels are dedicated for the corresponding outbound truck $o1$ with the deadline at the end of period $dl_{o1} = 10$. Accordingly, all parcels would arrive at the outbound before the deadline. The second inbound truck $i2$ arriving at the beginning of period $t2$ only unloads parcels for a corresponding outbound truck $o2$ with the deadline in period $dl_{o2} = 9$. Here, only 80% of parcels would arrive on time. For a third truck $i3$ with the same corresponding outbound deadline $dl_{o2} = 9$ that is scheduled to start unloading in period $t1$ only 90% of parcels would be loaded before the deadline. Assuming that 10 parcels from inbound truck $i1$ are designated for outbound $o1$, i.e. $ship_{i1,o1} = 10$, this would result in $uf_{i1,t1,o1} = 1 \cdot 10 = 10$. Further, if 10 parcels from the inbounds $i2$ and $i3$ are designated for $o2$, i.e. $ship_{i2,o2} = 10$ and $ship_{i3,o2} = 10$, the result would be $uf_{i2,t2,o2} = 0.8 \cdot 10 = 8$ and $uf_{i3,t1,o2} = 0.9 \cdot 10 = 9$ parcels without delay, respectively.

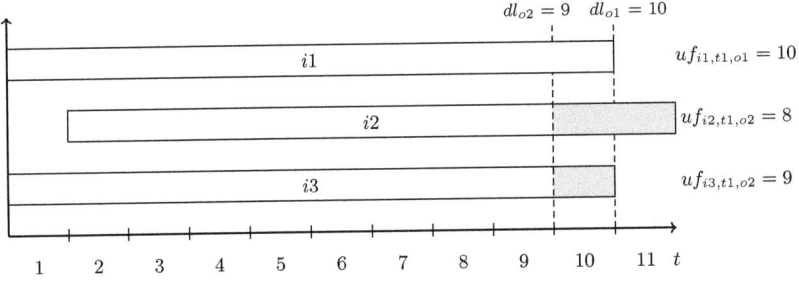

Figure 4.5.: Exemplary calculation of uf_{ito}

The model is applied to determine an optimal inbound truck schedule, i.e., to answer the question whether an inbound truck i should be scheduled at the beginning of period t or not, represented by the binary decision variable y_{it}.

In order to reduce the time horizon used in the model, the period after the last deadline, i.e. $T = max_{o \in \mathcal{O}}[dl_o] + 1$, is assumed to be a dummy period. In the last period, the capacity restrictions of the conveyors and the doors are relaxed. Thus, all inbound trucks that are not (fully) unloaded until the deadline are scheduled to be unloaded in this period. In all likelihood, the resulting schedule is not directly applicable to a real-world-setting. However, with regard to the objective function value, all parcels unloaded in or after the last deadline are tardy, no matter how late they are unloaded. This aspect does not have an influence on the realizability of the plan. To generate a plan that includes all inbound trucks and the periods after the last deadline in a post-processing step, the inbound trucks can be allocated to specific doors and the remaining inbound trucks arbitrarily scheduled in the periods after the last deadline. Table 4.2 summarizes the notation.

Table 4.2.: Notation of the PHSP-LCC-fix

Indices and (ordered) sets	
$i, j \in \mathcal{I}$	inbound trucks $\mathcal{I} = \{1, \dots, I\}$
$o \in \mathcal{O}$	outbound trucks $\mathcal{O} = \{1, \dots, O\}$
$k \in \mathcal{K}$	conveyor belts $\mathcal{K} = \{1, \dots, K\}$
$t, \tau \in \mathcal{T}$	periods $\mathcal{T} = \{1, \dots, T\}$
$o \in O_k \subseteq \mathcal{O}$	subset of outbound trucks connected by conveyor belt k
$t \in T_i \subseteq \mathcal{T}$	available periods for inbound truck i with $\mathcal{T}_i = \{at_i, \dots, T\}$

Parameters	
at_i	arrival time of inbound truck i
bl_o	total number of parcels in outbound o
d_i	unloading duration of inbound truck i
dl_o	deadline of outbound truck o
lr_{ik}	rate of parcels in inbound truck i designated for conveyor k per period
U	number of inbound doors
uf_{ito}	number of non-delayed parcels for outbound truck o if inbound truck i is scheduled at period t
r_k	capacity of conveyor k
$ship_{io}$	parcels for outbound truck o in inbound truck i

Decision variables	
y_{it}	$= \begin{cases} 1, & \text{if inbound truck } i \text{ is scheduled at the beginning of period } t \\ 0, & \text{otherwise} \end{cases}$

According to the classification scheme of truck scheduling problems at cross docking hubs by Boysen and Fliedner (2010) as illustrated on in Chapter 3 on page 19, the problem can be described as $[E|a_j, t_j = 0, \overline{d}_o, fix, \bar{r}_k | \sum U_o]$. Here, E refers to the exclusive usage of gates as inbounds or outbounds. The inbound trucks arrive throughout the planning horizon (a_j), transfer times are neglected $(t_j = 0)$, outbound trucks have deadlines (dl_o) and leave the hub at the deadlines (fix). As the objective, the number of parcels arriving on time is maximized which is equivalent to minimizing the number of tardy parcels. The novel extensions to the classification scheme are limited conveyor capacities as indicated by $\bar{r}_k$.

Time-indexed mathematical model of the PHSP-LCC-fix

The PHSP-LCC-fix can be formalized as a linear mixed-integer program as follows.

Time-indexed model for the PHSP-LCC-fix

$$max \; Z = \sum_{i \in \mathcal{I}} \sum_{t \in \mathcal{T} \setminus \{T\}} y_{it} \cdot \sum_{o \in O} u f_{ito} \qquad (4.3)$$

subject to

$$\sum_{i \in \mathcal{I}} \sum_{\tau = \max(at_i, t - d_i + 1)}^{t} y_{i\tau} \leq U \qquad \forall t \in \mathcal{T} \setminus \{T\} \qquad (4.4)$$

$$\sum_{i \in \mathcal{I}} \sum_{\tau = \max(at_i, t - d_i + 1)}^{t} y_{i\tau} \cdot lr_{ik} \leq r_k \qquad \forall t \in \mathcal{T} \setminus \{T\}, k \in \mathcal{K} \qquad (4.5)$$

$$\sum_{t \in \mathcal{T}_i} y_{it} = 1 \qquad \forall i \in \mathcal{I} \qquad (4.6)$$

$$y_{it} \in \{0, 1\} \qquad \forall i \in \mathcal{I}, t \in \mathcal{T}_i \qquad (4.7)$$

The objective function (4.3) maximizes the total number of parcels arriving on time. Inequalities (4.4) restrict the number of inbound trucks that can be unloaded at the same time to the number of inbound gates at the facility U for each period t with the exception of the last (dummy) period T. In each time period t, all currently unloaded inbound trucks i are considered and thus all inbound trucks i starting their unloading processes in the time interval between $t - d_i + 1$ and t. Constraints (4.5) enforce the capacity constraints of each conveyor k as the parcel flows from the currently unloaded inbound trucks lr_{ik} must not exceed the conveyor capacity r_k. Constraints (4.6) ensure that the unloading process of each inbound truck i is started exactly once after its arrival in period at_i using the time periods available to inbound $\mathcal{T}_i$. Note that inbound trucks can also be scheduled in the dummy period T. As the dummy period lies after the last deadline, all parcel loaded to an inbound truck that starts unloading in the dummy period are already delayed. Hence, they do not influence the objective function value. An equivalent formulation would allow trucks to be left unscheduled by substituting the equal sign with a less or equal sign. Leaving trucks unscheduled would lead to the same number of tardy parcels. To assure a higher degree of comparability with the models including controllable unloading speeds of the following sections, the shown approach is selected. Lastly, constraints (4.7) define the decision variables as binary.

Exemplary application of the time-indexed PHSP-LCC-fix

To illustrate an exemplary application of the model, a U-shaped hub with eight inbound doors $U1$ to $U8$ and 27 outbound doors $o1$ to $o27$ connected by four conveyors $k1$ to $k4$ as shown in Figure 1.1 on page 2 is studied. The exemplary hub is designed after an existing medium-sized parcel hub observed in practice. A total of 19 inbound trucks $i1$ to $i19$ containing 650 parcels each have to be processed and consequentially 12350 parcels are transferred in total. Each inbound truck is unloaded with a fixed rate of 65 parcels per five minutes and a maximum of 85 parcels can be transported concurrently on each conveyor every five minutes. The period length in the model is set to five minutes. Thus, the unloading rate and capacities also reference a time frame of five minutes. All outbound deadlines are scattered between 140 and 170 minutes. Figure 4.6 shows the optimal truck schedule and resulting conveyor utilization when solving the problem with the standard solver Gurobi.

The optimized schedule leads to 9600 parcels without delay and a makespan of 250 minutes for processing all inbound trucks. When examining the schedule closer, we can observe that only 5 out of the available 8 inbound gates are used whereas the maximum capacity on each conveyor is reached at least once. Thus, the conveyors constitute the bottleneck of the system. The conveyors are not utilized evenly and conveyor $k3$ shows the highest utilization. However, even conveyor $k3$ is not fully utilized in the later time periods. It is observable, that fixed unloading speeds limit the potential number of concurrently unloaded inbound trucks as some gates are never utilized. One option to better utilize the gates and conveyor capacities and increase the number of parcels without delay is to allow controllable unloading speeds. Controllable unloading speeds are promising option as they allow for a greater degree of flexibility and extend the solution space. Before discussing the opportunities of controllable unloading speeds more closely, a mathematical model for the PHSP-LCC-fix based on the interval scheduling approach is presented in the following section.

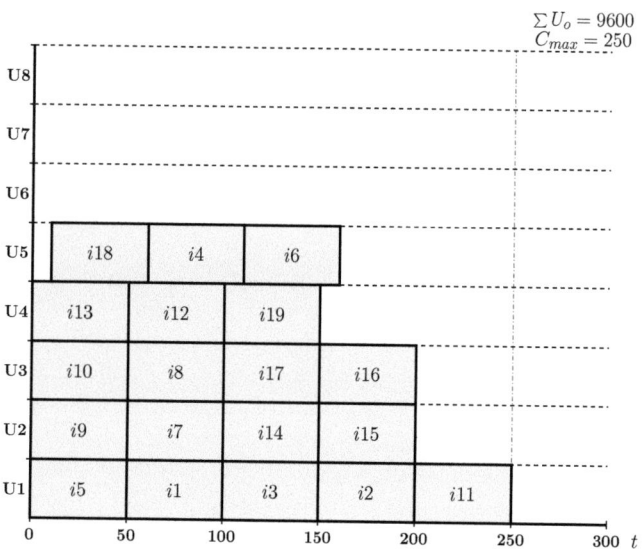

(a) Optimized schedule

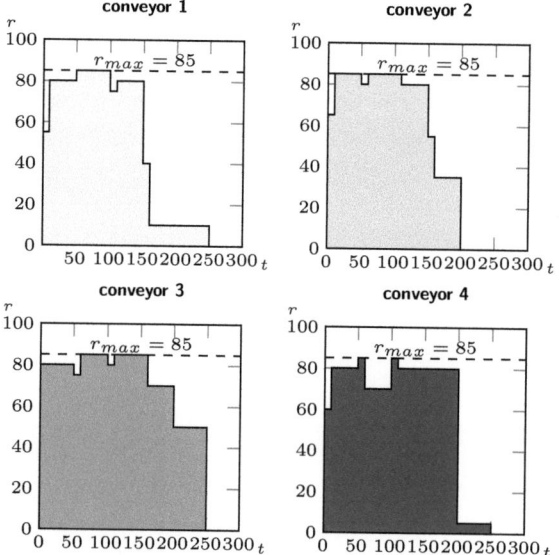

(b) Optimized conveyor utilisation

Figure 4.6.: Truck schedule and conveyor utilization for the PHSP-LCC-
flex

4.2.2. The interval-based PHSP-LCC-fix

Assumptions and notation

Different truck scheduling problems at cross docks have already been formulated as interval scheduling problems, for example by Boysen et al. (2017) and Tadumadze et al. (2019). The formulation of truck scheduling problems as an interval scheduling problem especially lends itself to applications where trucks can be processed in different modes of execution[3] as is the case for the problem setting with controllable unloading speeds. To also compare the time-indexed formulation of the PHSP-LCC-fix with an interval-based approach, the following section illustrates the assumptions and notation for the interval-based formulation of the PHSP-LCC-fix.

When applying an interval-based approach to the truck scheduling problem, the precise definition of intervals constitutes the basis of the formulation.[4] The set of intervals $m \in \mathcal{M}$ has to include all those time slices of the planning horizon that represent feasible unloading time frames for at least one of the inbound trucks $i \in \mathcal{I}$. To define those intervals, the length and start of each interval has to be defined. Here, the time horizon is discretized into distinct points in time. These times represent a finite number of possible valid starting times of at least one of the inbound trucks. The number of intervals is mainly dependent on the number of provided possible starting times. The length of the intervals is defined as every possible unloading duration d_i out of all inbound trucks. The subset $\mathcal{MJ}_i \subseteq \mathcal{M}$ defines all available intervals for inbound truck i and thus includes all intervals that start after the arrival time at_i of the inbound truck and have the same length as the unloading time d_i of the inbound.

An exemplary definition of intervals for a problem setting with a time horizon of $T = 4$ periods, two inbound trucks $I = \{1, 2\}$ with unloading times $d_1 = 2$ and $d_2 = 3$ as well as arrival times $at_1 = 1$ and $at_2 = 0$ at the end of the respective periods is illustrated in Figure 4.7.

Here, inbound $i = 1$ can only be processed in intervals $\mathcal{MJ}_1 = \{2, 3\}$ since these intervals are after the arrival of the inbound truck and possess the same length as the unloading time of the truck. Accordingly, inbound $i2$ can be unloaded in the intervals $\mathcal{MJ}_1 = \{4, 5\}$ since its unloading

---

[3]Boysen et al. (2017, p. 727).
[4]Kolen et al. (2007, p. 533).

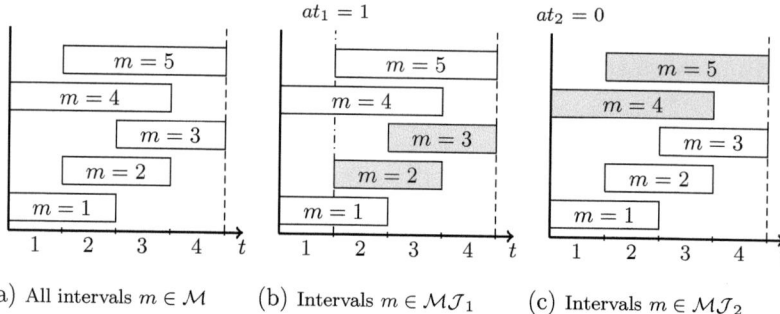

(a) All intervals $m \in \mathcal{M}$ (b) Intervals $m \in \mathcal{MJ}_1$ (c) Intervals $m \in \mathcal{MJ}_2$

Figure 4.7.: Exemplary interval definition

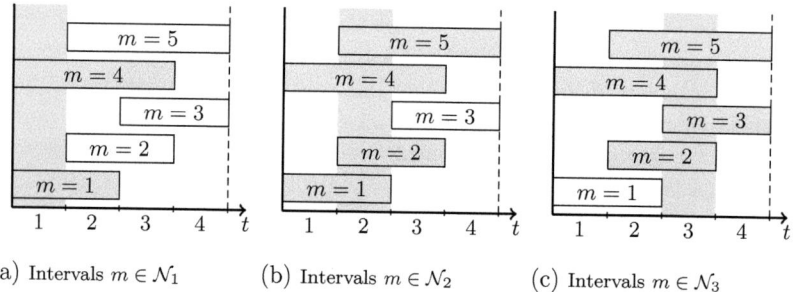

(a) Intervals $m \in \mathcal{N}_1$ (b) Intervals $m \in \mathcal{N}_2$ (c) Intervals $m \in \mathcal{N}_3$

Figure 4.8.: Exemplary relationship between intervals and periods

time $d_2 = 3$ and $at_2 = 0$.

An inbound truck i can be assigned to all intervals that lie after its arrival time at_i. All available inbound trucks at time period t are included in the subset $\mathcal{J}_t \subseteq \mathcal{I}$. Further, to model the gate and conveyor capacity in each period, the subset $\mathcal{N}_t \subseteq \mathcal{M}$ is introduced to indicate which intervals are active in a specific time period t. Figure 4.8 exemplifies the relationship between intervals and periods.

With reference to the example, the active intervals in period $t = 1$ are $\mathcal{N}_t = \{1, 4\}$. With the information which interval is active at period $t = 1$, the conveyor and gate utilization if inbound trucks are assigned to the intervals $\mathcal{N}_t = \{1, 4\}$ can be calculated.

To determine the number of parcels arriving on time, a parameter similar to uf_{ito} as shown in Formula (4.2) on page 39 is defined. Here, the parameter um_{mo} indicates the share of parcels arriving on time for outbound o, if an inbound truck is assigned to interval m as illustrated in the following formula:

$$um_{mo} = \begin{cases} 1, & st_m \leq dl_o - di_m \\ \frac{dl_o - st_m}{di_m}, & dl_o - di_m < st_m < dl_o \\ 0, & st_m \geq dl_o \end{cases} \qquad (4.8)$$

The deadline dl_o lies after the end of an interval m if deadline dl_o minus the length di_m of interval m is greater than its starting time. In other words, the end of the interval lies before the deadline. In this case, all parcels dedicated for outbound o arrive in time. If the deadline lies after the start but before the end of interval m, only a fraction of parcels are without delay. Since the unloading speed is assumed to be constant, the share of parcels arriving on time can be calculated by dividing the time between the start of the interval and the deadline $dl_o - st_m$ by the interval length di_m. For the third case, if the start of an interval lies after the deadline, all parcels are tardy.

Again, the goal is to determine the truck schedule that maximizes the number of parcels arriving on time and does not violate the restrictions imposed by the conveyor capacity and number of gates. The central decision is the assignment of inbound trucks i to an interval m as represented by the binary decision variables z_{im}. The notation is summarized in Table 4.3.

Interval-based mathematical model of the PHSP-LCC-fix

The model for the interval-based formulation of the PHSP-LCC-fix is formally defined as follows.

Table 4.3.: Additional notation of the interval-based PHSP-LCC-fix

Indices and (ordered) sets	
$i \in \mathcal{I}$	inbound trucks $\mathcal{I} = \{1, \dots, I\}$
$m \in \mathcal{M}$	intervals $\mathcal{M} = \{1, \dots, M\}$
$N_t \subseteq \mathcal{M}$	active intervals at period t
$MJ_i \subseteq \mathcal{M}$	available intervals for inbound truck i
$i \in J_t \subseteq \mathcal{I}$	available inbound trucks in period t

Parameters	
lk_{ik}	number of parcels in inbound truck i designated for conveyor k
st_m	starting period of interval m
di_m	length of interval m
um_{mo}	percentage of non-delayed parcels for outbound truck o if a truck is scheduled at interval m

Decision variables	
z_{im}	$= \begin{cases} 1, & \text{if inbound truck } i \text{ is assigned to interval } m \\ 0, & \text{otherwise} \end{cases}$

Interval-based model for the PHSP-LCC-fix

$$max \; Z = \sum_{o \in \mathcal{O}} \sum_{i \in \mathcal{I}} \sum_{m \in \mathcal{MJ}_i} z_{im} \cdot ship_{io} \cdot um_{mo} \qquad (4.9)$$

subject to

$$\sum_{m \in \mathcal{MJ}_i} z_{im} \leq 1 \qquad\qquad \forall i \in \mathcal{I} \qquad\qquad (4.10)$$

$$\sum_{i \in \mathcal{J}_t} \sum_{m \in \mathcal{N}_t \cap \mathcal{MJ}_i} z_{im} \frac{lk_{ik}}{di_m} \leq r_k \qquad \forall t \in \mathcal{T}, k \in \mathcal{K} \qquad (4.11)$$

$$\sum_{i \in \mathcal{J}_t} \sum_{m \in \mathcal{N}_t \cap \mathcal{MJ}_i} z_{im} \leq U \qquad \forall t \in \mathcal{T} \qquad\qquad (4.12)$$

$$z_{im} \in \{0, 1\} \qquad\qquad \forall i \in \mathcal{I}, m \in \mathcal{MJ}_i \qquad (4.13)$$

The objective function (4.9) maximizes the total number of parcels without delay. Here, the total number of parcels without delay is calculated by multiplying the share of parcels that arrive at the outbound trucks before the respective deadline with the total number of parcels that are loaded to the inbound trucks. Constraints (4.10) state that each inbound can only be assigned to a single interval and thus is only unloaded once. The formulation allows some inbound trucks to remain unscheduled. Equivalent to the time-indexed formulation, all the remaining inbound trucks can be unloaded after the last deadline arbitrarily without any impact on the total number of parcels without delay. Inequalities (4.11) define the capacity restrictions on each conveyor in each period. To connect the periods and intervals, the intersection $m \in \mathcal{N}_t \cap \mathcal{MJ}_i$ is used. It indicates which intervals are currently active in the respective period and only considers the trucks that are already available for unloading. Similarly, the gate capacity is formulated using (4.30) which only considers currently active intervals and available inbound trucks, too. Lastly, constraints (4.13) define the decision variables as binary for all the intervals available to the respective inbound truck.

Exemplary application of the interval-based PHSP-LCC-fix

The resulting schedule and conveyor utilization when applying the interval based formulation to the exemplary instance with 19 inbound trucks and 27 outbound trucks illustrated in Section 4.2.1 on page 43 is shown in Figure 4.9.

The resulting schedule, capacity utilization and objective function value are identical for the interval-based formulation in comparison to the time-indexed model. This indicates that both model formulations generate equivalent results for the same instance. The differences with regard to the computational performance are discussed in Section 4.5.

4.3. Model formulations for the PHSP-LCC with Controllable Unloading Speeds (PHSP-LCC-flex)

4.3.1. Incorporating flexibility in the unloading process

McWilliams et al. (2005) illustrate specific circumstances in parcel hubs where the managers responsible for the parcel flows may decide to slow down the unloading speed by reassigning workers of individual inbound

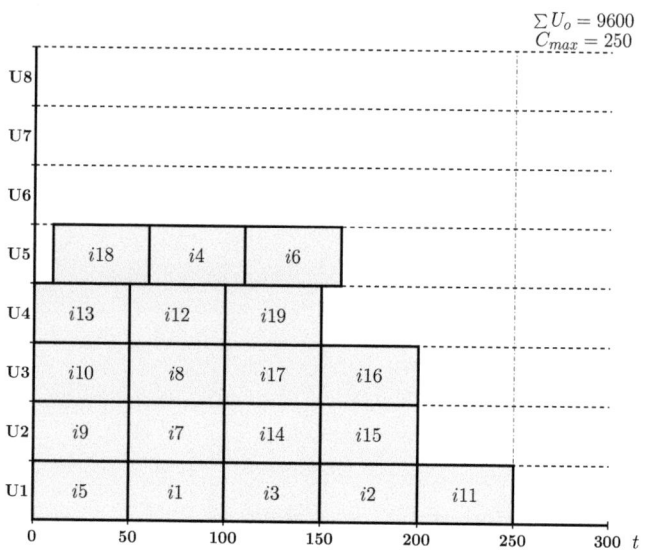

(a) Optimized schedule

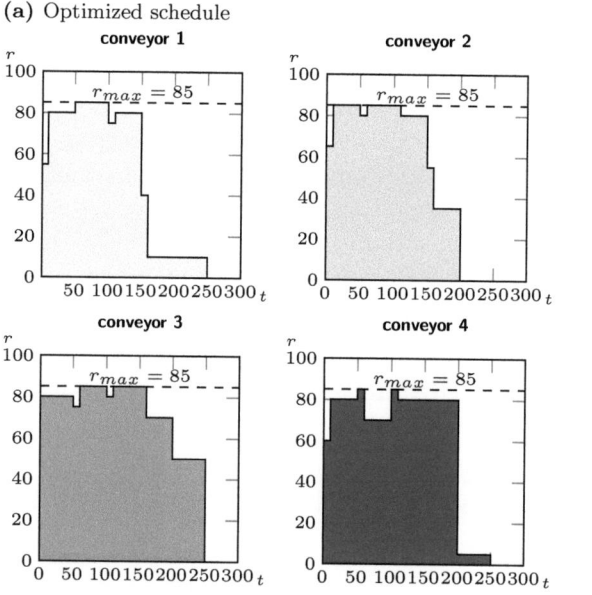

(b) Optimized conveyor utilization

Figure 4.9.: Truck schedule and conveyor utilization for the Interval-Based PHSP-LCC-fix

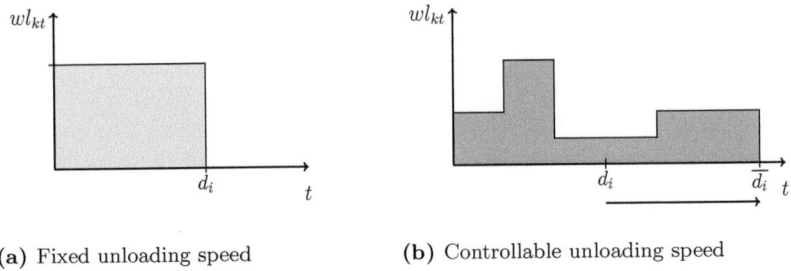

(a) Fixed unloading speed   (b) Controllable unloading speed

Figure 4.10.: Exemplary resource profile for fixed and controllable unloading speed

trucks to control the workload on specific conveyors that currently constitute the bottleneck of the system. This way, workload peaks on the bottleneck conveyors can potentially be flattened and congestion avoided. Further, unused capacities on other conveyors are unlocked since the reassigned workers can unload inbound trucks that contain shipments dedicated for those conveyors. The effects of slowing down unloading speeds are illustrated in Figure 4.10 for the unloading process of a single truck.

Slowing down the unloading speed of an individual truck i increases its unloading time d_i whereas its induced workload wl_{kt} on conveyor k decreases at a given period t. Conceptually, the set of trucks that can be unloaded simultaneously without exceeding conveyor capacities is now only limited by the number of available inbound doors and the respective unloading rate. As a result, flexibility in the unloading speed opens up optimization opportunities with regard to the usage of conveyor utilization.

The previously mentioned approach by McWilliams et al. (2005) illustrates unloading speed flexibility but does not explicitly include the option to influence the unloading process in the optimization model. With regard to cross dock scheduling literature, Tadumadze et al. (2019) incorporate flexibility in unloading speeds by integrating operational personnel planning into the truck scheduling problem but do not consider limited conveyor capacities. Corsten et al. (2020) include tactical shift planning in truck scheduling decisions. Similarly, Ladier and Alpan (2015) include staff timetabling decisions and focus on influence on the internal workload in the truck scheduling problem.

With regard to the problem structure, the Resource-Constrained Project Scheduling Problem with flexible Resource Profiles (FRCPSP) as described by Naber and Kolisch (2014) has similar properties. The resource usage of a job is modeled as a decision and can be influenced by shortening or expanding the duration of a job similar to the decision of shortening and lengthening the unloading process of inbound trucks for the truck scheduling problem at parcel hubs. However, the specific circumstances in parcel hubs such as the transfer on conveyors and different handling steps of the unloading process cannot be transferred into the framework of the FRCPSP. Further, the assumption that the resource usage while unloading a truck varies throughout its execution differs from the basic assumptions of the FRCPSP which assumes constant resource usage throughout the execution of a job.

The field of machine scheduling with controllable processing times is another similar problem setting and illustrated in Shabtay and Steiner (2007) and Cheng et al. (1996). Again, a scarce resource is employed to shorten or lengthen the duration of a job as in the FRCPSP. For the truck scheduling problem at cross docks, conveyor capacities would be interpreted as a renewable resource used to shorten or lengthen the unloading process. However, the resource consumption for each job is again assumed to be constant contrary to the truck scheduling problem at parcel hubs. For the scheduling problem at parcel hubs, we assume that the resource consumption may vary throughout the execution of a job and is controllable.

Thus, a further research question posed in this work is how flexibility in the unloading process can improve the performance of parcel hub operations.

4.3.2. The time-indexed PHSP-LCC-flex

Assumptions and notation

If we assume that the unloading speeds of the inbound trucks can be controlled, alterations of the mathematical model are required. All other basic assumptions from Section 4.1 on page 31 still hold. The additionally needed notation for the **P**arcel **H**ub **S**cheduling **P**roblem with **L**imited

Conveyor Capacity and **Flex**ible Unloading Speeds (PHSP-LCC-flex) is presented in Table 4.4. Since we now assume that the unloading speed is controllable, we have to define the maximum unloading speed of parcels per period at a single door which is represented by x_i^{max}. Here, the basic assumption is that the maximum unloading speed corresponds to the standard unloading speed when considering fixed speeds. Thus, the basic idea is allowing the unloading process to be slowed in order to react to workload peaks.

Additionally, the total load l_i of inbound truck i can be calculated as follows:

$$l_i = \sum_{o \in \mathcal{O}} ship_{io} \qquad (4.14)$$

Further, $\mathcal{I}_t \subseteq \mathcal{I}$ defines the subset of inbound trucks i that are available in period t. Thus, it encompasses all inbound trucks with an arrival time at_i before period t.

By introducing the decision on the unloading speeds additional decision variables are needed. Instead of using the binary variable y_{it} defining the period the unloading process of an inbound starts, the binary variable z_{it} is introduced being 1 in *each* period t an inbound truck i is located at a door. The continuous variable $x_{it} \geq 0$ now represents the number of parcels that are unloaded in period t from inbound truck i. Thus, it can be interpreted as the unloading speed. It could be argued that x_{it} should rather be modeled as an integer variable as the individual parcels are separate entities. However, aggregating parcels using a continuous decision variable only results in minor inaccuracies of the model and renders it much more mathematically tractable. Accordingly, x_{it} is modeled as a continuous variable.

As the unloading speed is now flexible, some notation from the PHSP-LCC-fix is obsolete for the PHSP-LCC-flex. The PHSP-LCC-fix assumes a fixed unloading rate lk_{ik} that is now substituted by the decision variable x_{it}. Further, the parameter uf_{ito} cannot be used anymore, since it assumes a specific unloading duration for each inbound truck and is thus disregarded for the PHSP-LCC-flex.

With reference to the classification scheme by Boysen and Fliedner (2010), the problem can be defined as $[E|a_j, t_j = 0, \overline{d_o}, fix, \overline{r}_k, p_i = var| \sum U_o]$. In comparison to the PHSP-LCC-fix, the term $p_i = var$ is added which refers to controllable unloading speeds. The other basic assumptions remain unaltered.

Table 4.4.: Additional notation of the PHSP-LCC-flex

Indices and (ordered) sets	
$i \in \mathcal{I}_t \subseteq \mathcal{I}$	inbound trucks i available in period t with $\mathcal{I}_t = \{at_i, \ldots, T\}$

Parameters	
l_i	number of parcels in inbound truck i
x_i^{max}	maximum number of unloaded parcels each time period

Decision variables	
$x_{it} \geq 0$	number of parcels unloaded in period t from inbound truck i
z_{it}	$= \begin{cases} 1, & \text{if inbound truck } i \text{ is located at a door in period } t \\ 0, & \text{otherwise} \end{cases}$

Time-indexed mathematical model of the PHSP-LCC-flex

The mixed-integer model for the time-indexed PHSP-LCC-flex is formally defined as follows.

Time-indexed model for the PHSP-LCC-flex

$$max\ Z = \sum_{o \in \mathcal{O}} \sum_{t=1}^{dl_o-1} \sum_{i \in \mathcal{I}_t} x_{it} \cdot \frac{ship_{io}}{l_i} \qquad (4.15)$$

subject to

$$\sum_{i \in \mathcal{I}_t} z_{it} \leq U \qquad\qquad \forall t \in \mathcal{T} \setminus \{T\} \qquad (4.16)$$

$$\sum_{i \in \mathcal{I}_t} x_{it} \leq r_k \qquad\qquad \forall k \in \mathcal{K}, \forall t \in \mathcal{T} \setminus \{T\} \quad (4.17)$$

$$\sum_{t \in \mathcal{T}_i} x_{it} = l_i \qquad\qquad \forall i \in I \qquad (4.18)$$

$$x_{it} \leq z_{it} \cdot x_i^{max} \qquad\qquad \forall i \in \mathcal{I}, \forall t \in \mathcal{T}_i \setminus \{T\} \quad (4.19)$$

$$\sum_{\tau=at_i}^{t} z_{i\tau} \leq t \cdot (1 + z_{it} - z_{it+1}) \qquad \forall i \in \mathcal{I}, \forall t \in \mathcal{T}_i \setminus \{at_i, T\}$$
$$(4.20)$$

$$\sum_{\tau=t}^{T} z_{i\tau} \leq (T - t + 1) \cdot (1 + z_{it} - z_{it-1}) \quad \forall i \in \mathcal{I}, \forall t \in \mathcal{T}_i \setminus \{at_i, T\}$$
$$(4.21)$$

$$z_{it} \in \{0,1\} \qquad\qquad \forall i \in \mathcal{I}, \forall t \in \mathcal{T}_i \qquad (4.22)$$

$$x_{it} \geq 0 \qquad\qquad \forall i \in \mathcal{I}, \forall t \in \mathcal{T}_i \qquad (4.23)$$

The objective function (4.15) again maximizes the number of parcels without delay. Here, $\frac{ship_{io}}{l_i}$ refers to the fraction of parcels from inbound truck i that are designated for outbound truck o. The fraction of parcels from inbound truck i that are designated for outbound truck o has to be included in the objective function as the outbound deadlines differ from each other and each inbound i includes parcels for a multitude of outbound trucks. Restrictions (4.16) represent the limitations due to the available number of doors. Constraints (4.17) define the conveyor capacity. Both limitations are excluded for the last (dummy) period T. Constrains (4.18) assure that parcels of each inbound truck i are actually unloaded between the arrival at_i of the inbound truck i and the dummy period T. Parcels can only be unloaded from an inbound truck i if the truck is located at a door in the respective period t ($z_{it} = 1$) due to restrictions (4.19). Constraints (4.20) restrict $z_{i\tau}$ to 0 for all *former* periods $\tau \leq t$ if truck i was assigned to a door in period $t + 1$ ($z_{it} = 0$ and $z_{i,t+1} = 1$). Analogously, constraints (4.21) force $z_{i\tau}$ to 0 for periods $\tau \geq t$ after the truck was removed from the door in the previous period $t - 1$ ($z_{i,t-1} = 1$ and $z_{it} = 0$). In combination, these constraints define an uninterrupted assignment of the inbound truck at a door. An inbound truck can potentially be located at door ($z_{it} = 1$) while not being unloaded ($x_{it} = 0$) in that time period. The formulation is similar to the on/off event-based formulation of the resource-constrained project scheduling problem as for example in Koné et al. (2011). Constraints (4.22) and (4.23) define the variable types.

Exemplary application of the time-indexed PHSP-LCC-flex

For an exemplary application of the formulation, the reference hub with 19 inbound trucks and 27 outbound trucks from Section 4.2.1 on page 43 is inspected again and the results in comparison to the PHSP-LCC-fix are presented. Figure 4.11 shows the optimal truck schedule determined with the standard solver Gurobi and the resulting conveyor utilization for the PHSP-LCC-flex.

By allowing unloading time flexibility, the number of parcels without delay can be increased from 9600 to 10264 parcels. Further, the makespan decreases from 250 to 220 minutes. The individual unloading times of the inbound trucks differs widely as observable in the optimized truck schedule. Some inbound trucks as for example i5 are unloaded at maximum unloading speed and take only 50 minutes while other such as i3 take up to 150 minutes. Note that fluctuations of the conveyor utilization at the end of the planning horizon after the last deadline are mostly arbitrary as they have no impact on the objective function value. In contrast to the results for the PHSP-LCC with fixed unloading speeds, all inbound doors are utilized to unload inbound trucks. This can be attributed to the flexibility in the unloading times, since the increased flexibility allows the concurrent unloading of trucks that could not have been unloaded together due to the limited conveyor capacities under the assumption of fixed unloading speeds. Further, the conveyor utilization is generally higher and the bottleneck conveyor 3 is now nearly fully utilized. The example shows that by allowing flexibility in the unloading time the conveyor capacity is used more efficiently and the number of parcels without delay can be increased significantly. Somewhat counter-

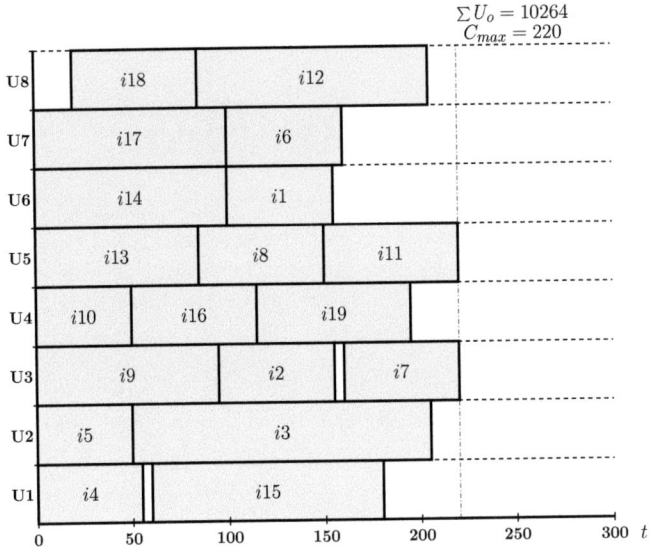

(a) Optimized schedule

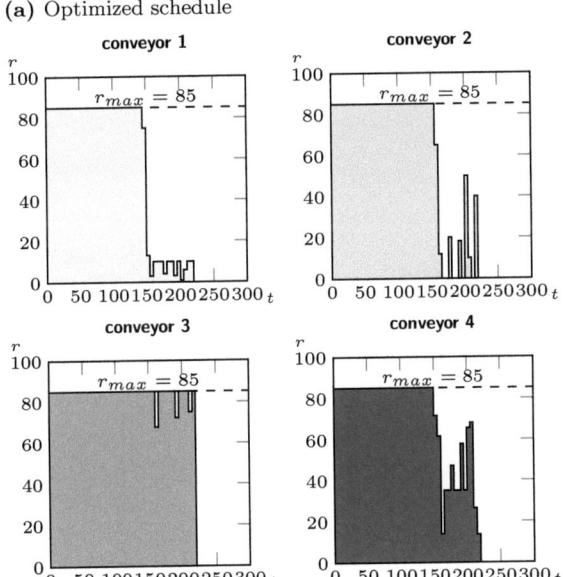

(b) Optimized conveyor utilisation

Figure 4.11.: Truck schedule and conveyor utilization for the PHSP-LCC-flex

intuitively, it becomes apparent that slowing down the local work speed of the unloading process can increase the work speed of the overall process.

4.3.3. The interval-based PHSP-LCC-flex

Assumptions and notation

As for the time-indexed formulation, the interval-based model of the PHSP-LCC is also extended by the option of controllable unloading speeds. Table 4.5 summarizes the notation for the interval-based PHSP-LCC with controllable unloading speeds. The remaining notation is taken from Table 4.3.

Table 4.5.: Additional notation of the Interval-Based PHSP-LCC-flex

Indices and (ordered) sets	
$t \in \mathcal{T}_i \subseteq \mathcal{T}$	available periods for inbound truck i with
$M^- \subseteq \mathcal{M}$	subset of intervals ending before the last deadline

Parameters	
d_i	standard unloading duration of inbound i
l_i	total number of parcels in inbound i
x_i^{max}	maximum number of unloaded parcels each period

Decision variables	
$x_{it} \geq 0$	number of parcels unloaded from inbound truck i in period t

As for the interval-based PHSP-LCC-fix, defining the intervals for the interval-based PHSP-LCC-flex is crucial for the model formulation. Under the assumption of fixed unloading speeds the intervals themselves and their length are clearly defined by the number of parcels in the inbound trucks and the standard (fixed) unloading speed. The standard unloading speed results in a fixed unloading duration and thus also a fixed interval length for each inbound. When formulating the problem assuming controllable unloading speeds, now the interval definition has to represent every feasible duration of the unloading process. Since one basic assumption is that the unloading speed can only be slowed down and not be sped up as illustrated in Section 4.3.1, the minimum interval length is the standard duration d_i. This reflects unloading an inbound

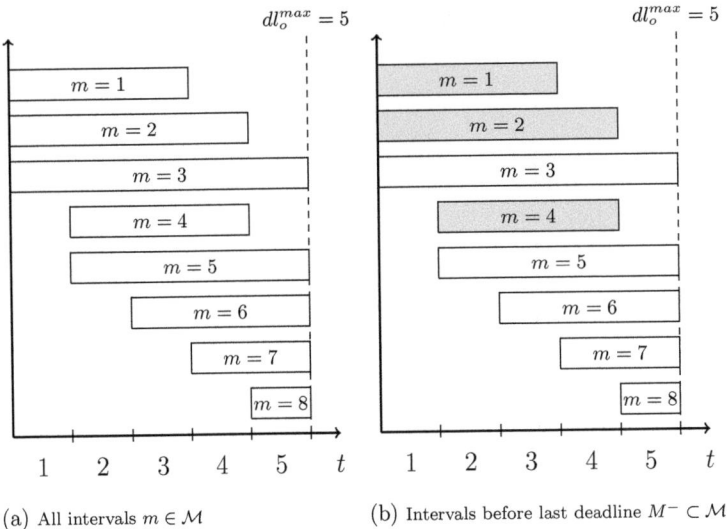

Figure 4.12.: Exemplary interval definition with variable length

truck with maximum speed. If the unloading process is slowed, however, the overall duration increases and thus intervals with a greater length are required. The longest interval spans the whole planning horizon and represents an inbound that starts the unloading process in the first period and stays at the gate until the last period.

Equivalent to the time-indexed formulation of the problem, all periods after the last deadline are irrelevant with regard to the objective function value. Hence, all intervals that lie fully after the last deadline do not have to be included. For intervals partially lying after the last deadline, the ending time can be set to the last deadline, since everything unloaded after the deadline does not influence the objective function value. Each interval ending at the last deadline represents all intervals with the same starting time and all ending times after the last deadline. Intervals ending strictly before the last deadline are denominated as the subset $\mathcal{M}^- \subseteq \mathcal{M}$. Figure 4.12 shows an exemplary depiction of the available intervals for a setting with standard unloading duration $d_i = 3$ and the last deadline at the end of the period $d_o^{max} = 5$.

The example shows that only the intervals $\mathcal{M}^- = \{1, 2, 4\}$ start and end strictly before the last deadline. If an inbound truck is assigned to these intervals, all parcels inside the truck have to be unloaded as one of the basic assumptions is that all inbound trucks are unloaded fully before they leave the gate. For the intervals $m \in \{3, 5, 6\}$ an inbound truck assigned to these intervals is potentially fully unloaded until the deadline since the interval length is at least as long as the standard unloading duration. Thus, on first glance it might seem reasonable to include these instances in $\mathcal{M}^-$. However, these intervals also represent all intervals with the same starting time and an arbitrary ending time after the last deadline. As a consequence, the condition of fully unloading the inbound trucks can be relaxed for those intervals as the unloading process has the potential to continue after the last deadline without influencing the objective function value. The length of the remaining intervals $m \in \{7, 8\}$ is shorter than the standard unloading duration and thus an inbound assigned to these intervals cannot be unloaded fully before the deadline and inevitably includes tardy parcels.

Further, the subset $\mathcal{T}_i$ represents all the periods available to inbound i. The objective is still to determine a truck schedule that does not exceed the gate or conveyor capacities with the goal of maximizing the number of parcels without delay. Since unloading speeds are controllable, the decision variable $x_{it} \geq 0$ representing the number of unloaded parcels from inbound truck i at time period t is introduced. Further, the binary decision variable z_{im} is 1, if inbound i is assigned to interval m and 0 otherwise.

Interval-based mathematical model of the PHSP-LCC-flex

The interval-based formulation of the PHSP-LCC-flex is formally defined as follows.

Interval-based model for the PHSP-LCC-flex

$$max \; Z = \sum_{o \in \mathcal{O}} \sum_{i \in \mathcal{I}} \sum_{t \in \mathcal{T}_i} x_{it} \cdot \frac{ship_{io}}{l_i} \tag{4.24}$$

subject to

$$\sum_{m \in \mathcal{M}} z_{im} = 1 \qquad \forall i \in \mathcal{I} \tag{4.25}$$

$$\sum_{t \in \mathcal{T}_i} x_{it} \geq \sum_{m \in \mathcal{M}^-} z_{im} \cdot l_i \qquad \forall i \in \mathcal{I} \tag{4.26}$$

$$\sum_{t \in \mathcal{T}_i} x_{it} \leq \sum_{m \in \mathcal{M}} z_{im} \cdot l_i \qquad \forall i \in \mathcal{I} \tag{4.27}$$

$$x_{it} \leq \sum_{m \in \mathcal{N}_t} z_{im} \cdot x_i^{max} \qquad \forall i \in \mathcal{I}, t \in \mathcal{T}_i \tag{4.28}$$

$$\sum_{i \in \mathcal{J}_t} x_{it} \cdot \frac{lk_{ik}}{l_i} \leq r_k \qquad \forall t \in \mathcal{T}, k \in \mathcal{K} \tag{4.29}$$

$$\sum_{i \in \mathcal{I}} \sum_{m \in \mathcal{N}_t} z_{im} \leq U \qquad \forall t \in \mathcal{T} \tag{4.30}$$

$$z_{im} \in \{0, 1\} \qquad \forall i \in \mathcal{I}, m \in \mathcal{M} \tag{4.31}$$

$$x_{it} \geq 0 \qquad \forall i \in \mathcal{I}, t \in \mathcal{T}_i \tag{4.32}$$

The goal is again to maximize the number of parcels without delay as defined by the objective function (4.24). Constraints (4.25) allow every inbound truck to be assigned to a single interval. An equivalent formulation would be substituting the equality sign with an less-or-equal sign. Then, not all trucks would have to be scheduled. As the number of non-delayed parcels is maximized, only those trucks that could only be scheduled after the last deadline would not be scheduled in this case. As those trucks do not influence the objective function, they could be scheduled arbitrarily in a post-processing step. Restrictions (4.26) state that all inbound trucks that are assigned to the intervals before the last deadline have to be fully unloaded. If a truck is assigned to an interval that includes the last deadline, they do not have to be fully unloaded as these intervals represent all intervals with the same starting time and an arbitrary end after the last deadline. Further, the number of parcels unloaded from an inbound truck can not exceed the total number of parcels in the inbound truck as defined in (4.27). With regard to the individual time periods, restrictions (4.28) limit the number of parcels that can be unloaded from an inbound trucks as dictated by the maximum unloading speed x_i^{max}. The conveyor capacity is modeled in constraints (4.29), the gate capacity in (4.30). Lastly, the binary integrality constraint (4.31) and the non-negativity constraint (4.32) define the decision variables.

Exemplary application of the interval-based PHSP-LCC-flex

The exemplary hub with 19 inbound trucks and 27 outbound trucks from Section 4.2.1 on page 43 is utilized again to illustrate the application of the interval-based PHSP-LCC-flex. Figure 4.13 shows the optimal truck schedule and corresponding resource utilization.

The resulting schedule leads to $\sum U_o = 10264$ non-delayed parcels just like the corresponding schedule of the time-indexed model as shown in Figure 4.11. Some of the inbound trucks are scheduled in different time intervals compared to the time-indexed model and the schedule length is slightly longer with $C_{max} = 230$. However, as the schedule length is not the chosen optimization criterion, both formulations are equivalent with regard to the objective function value and the solution space. More detailed insights into the computational performance of the approaches with controllable unloading speeds are presented in Section 4.5.

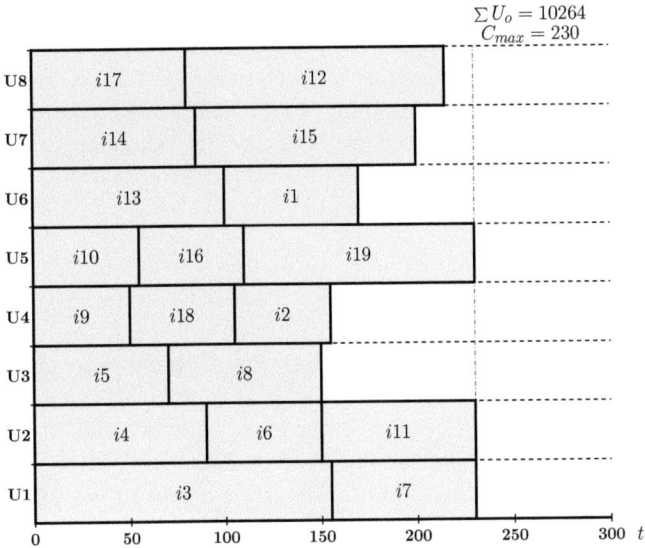

(a) Optimized schedule

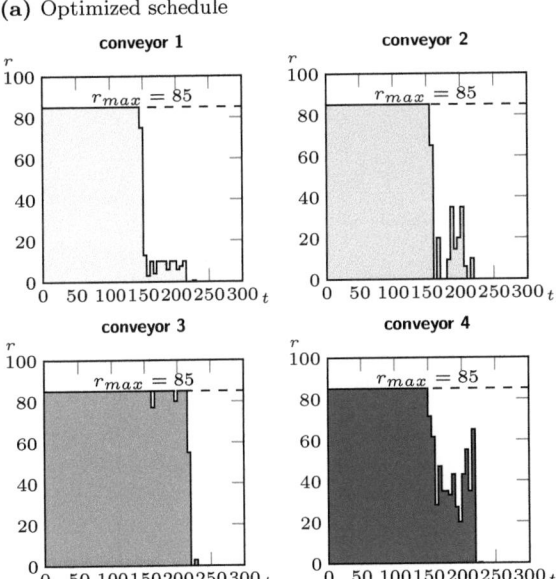

(b) Optimized conveyor utilization

Figure 4.13.: Truck schedule and conveyor utilization for the interval-based PHSP-LCC-flex

4.4. Computational complexity of the problem

To assess the computational complexity of the PHSP-LCC-flex and PHSP-LCC-fix, we first determine if we can represent an instance of the PHSP-LCC-fix as an instance of the PHSP-LCC-flex. We introduce a constraint that defines the minimum number of unloaded parcels in a period using the parameter x_i^{min} to the time-based formulation of the PHSP-LCC-flex.

$$x_{it} \geq z_{it} \cdot x_i^{min} \qquad\qquad \forall i \in \mathcal{I}, t \in \mathcal{T}_i \qquad (4.33)$$

If $x_i^{min} = 0$ the solution space of the PHSP-LCC-flex remains unchanged as the constraint is a redundant formulation of the non-negativity constraint for x_{it}. However, if $x_i^{min} = x_i^{max}$ the unloading speed of the inbound trucks is fixed to the standard unloading speed and all flexibility is excluded. Consequentially, we receive an instance of the PHSP-LCC-fix and if we can prove that the PHSP-LCC-fix is NP-hard, the PHSP-LCC-flex is also NP-hard.

To determine the nondeterministic polynomial time (NP)-hardness of the PHSP-LCC-fix, the problem of scheduling jobs on a single machine minimizing the total weighted tardiness of all jobs can be referenced. A similar approach can be found in Boysen et al. (2013) for a truck scheduling problem at cross docks with fixed departure times. The single machine job scheduling problem minimizing total weighted tardiness is defined as follows:[5]

For a given set of jobs $j \in J$ with processing times p'_j, due dates d'_j and weights w'_j find a schedule that minimizes the following function:

$$\sum_{j' \in J} w'_j \cdot max\{0, C_j - d'_j\} \qquad (4.34)$$

where C_j is the completion time of job j.

According to the Graham Notation,[6] the problem can be represented by the tuple $1||\sum w_j\, T_j$ and has been proven to be strongly NP-hard by Lawler (1977).

Representing an instance of $1||\sum w_j\, T_j$ as an instance of the PHSP-LCC-fix first involves assuming a hub with only a single gate and thus

---

[5]Emmons (1969, pp. 701-703).
[6]Graham et al. (1979, p. 288).

$U = 1$. The conveyor capacities are rendered irrelevant by setting $lr_{ik} = 0 \ \forall i \in \mathcal{I}, k \in \mathcal{K}$ or $r_k = \infty \ \forall k \in \mathcal{K}$. Each inbound truck i represents a job j. Further, an outbound truck o' is created for each period t. For the objective function, the value for $uf_{ito'}$ is set to zero for all outbounds except for the outbound o' that corresponds to the jobs deadline d'_j. For the deadline of job j, $uf_{jtd'_j}$ is calculated according to the following formula:

$$uf_{jtd'_j} = \begin{cases} 0, & t \le d'_j - p'_j \\ w_j \cdot (t + p'_j - d'_j), & \text{else} \end{cases} \tag{4.35}$$

This way, a tardy job j is penalized according to the weighted sum of periods it is processed after its deadline.

With the stated reduction, any instance of $1||\sum w_j \, T_j$ can be represented as an instance of the PHSP-LCC-fix and consequentially also as an instance of the PHSP-LCC-flex as stated above. As $1||\sum w_j \, T_j$ is proven to be strongly NP-hard, both the PHSP-LCC-fix and PHSP-LCC-flex are strongly NP-hard as well.

4.5. Numerical analysis of the PHSP-LCC

4.5.1. Instance generation for the PHSP-LCC

Instance generation scheme

To gain further insights concerning the structural properties and influence of specific instance characteristics for the PHSP-LCC, a numerical study utilizing test instances for different parcel hubs and operational settings is devised. The numerical analysis is based on two data sets that reference hubs of different sizes of practical relevance. The instances have already been used in Bugow and Kellenbrink (2023). One class of instances represents a smaller parcel hub with $|\mathcal{I}| = 19$ inbound trucks, $|\mathcal{O}| = 27$ outbound destinations and $|\mathcal{K}| = 4$ connecting conveyors. The second data set represents a larger hub with $|\mathcal{I}| = 36$ inbound trucks and $|\mathcal{O}| = 55$ outbound destinations connected by $|\mathcal{K}| = 5$ conveyors. Each conveyor serves a subset of all destinations. The subsets of destinations have about the same cardinality.

For both types of hubs a variety of operational settings relating to different levels of resource scarcity, deadline distribution and parcel compositions are designed. All inbound trucks i receive the same number of parcels with $l_i = 650$ and have a corresponding standard unloading time $d_i = 10$ periods for all instances. This refers to a maximum speed x_i^{max} of 65 $\frac{parcels}{period}$. The individual parcels are randomly assigned to a number of destinations represented by outbound trucks o according to the parameter $\alpha \in]0,1]$. The parameter determines the heterogeneity of the parcels inside the inbound trucks with regard to their destination. For a heterogeneity $\alpha = 1$, each inbound truck potentially includes parcels for all destinations. A heterogeneity $\alpha = 0.5$ refers to the case where the parcels are designated for 50% of destinations etc. To generate the parcel composition of each inbound, a random subset $\mathcal{O}_i^{sub} \subseteq \mathcal{O}$ with $\lceil |\mathcal{O}| \cdot \alpha \rceil$ elements is generated first.

$$\mathcal{O}_i^{sub} = \text{sample}(\mathcal{O}, \lceil |\mathcal{O}| \cdot \alpha \rceil) \qquad \forall i \in \mathcal{I} \qquad (4.36)$$

A randomly determined preliminary number of parcels $ship_{io}$ per destination o as defined by the following equation:

$$ship_{io}^{pre} = \text{rand}(0.5, 1.5) \cdot \frac{l_i}{|\mathcal{O}_i^{sub}|} \qquad \forall o \in \mathcal{O}_i^{sub}, \forall i \in \mathcal{I} \qquad (4.37)$$

Then, the preliminary values are adjusted to equal the total number of parcels l_i for each inbound truck. Thus, for each inbound truck the number of parcels for a random destination is decreased or increased until the total number of parcels $\sum_{o \in \mathcal{O}_i^{sub}} ship_{io}$ equals l_i. Algorithm 4.1 shows the generation procedure.

Algorithm 4.1: Generate inbound parcel composition

Input: α, i, O, l_i

Output: parcel composition $ship_{io}$

1   generate a random subset of outbounds
     $\mathcal{O}_i^{sub} = \text{sample}(\mathcal{O}, \lceil |\mathcal{O}| \cdot \alpha \rceil)$

2   **for** $o \in \mathcal{O}_i^{sub}$ **do**

3     $ship_{io} = \text{rand}(0.5, 1.5) \cdot \frac{l_i}{|\mathcal{O}_i^{sub}|}$

4   **while** $\sum_{o \in \mathcal{O}_i^{sub}} ship_{io} < l_i$ **do**

5   select random outbound $o \in \mathcal{O}_i^{sub}$

6     $ship_{io} = ship_{io} + 1$

7   **while** $\sum_{o \in \mathcal{O}_i^{sub}} ship_{io} > l_i$ **do**

8   select random outbound $o \in \mathcal{O}_i^{sub}$

9   **if** $ship_{io} > 0$ **then**

10       $ship_{io} = ship_{io} - 1$

The standard length of the time horizon is set to $T^{norm} = 36$. T^{norm} refers to a preliminary length of the time horizon and the actual time horizon is potentially longer depending on the deadline distribution. With a period length of 5 minutes, the standard planning horizon has a length of 180 minutes. To set the deadline dl_o of each outbound destination, the parameter $\mu \in [0, 1]$ is used.

$$dl_o = \lceil \text{rand}(1 - \mu, 1 + \mu) \cdot T^{norm} \rceil \qquad \forall o \in \mathcal{O} \qquad (4.38)$$

The formula allows for deadlines after the standard length of the time horizon T^{norm}. Thus, the actual length of the time horizon T is later set to one period after the last deadline $dl_o^{max} = \max_{o \in \mathcal{O}} dl_o$.

To investigate hubs with different levels of resource scarcity, namely conveyor scarcity and gate scarcity, a factor for the resource scarcity of individual instances is introduced. First, a lower limit for the conveyor capacity r_k^{LB} is calculated. To calculate r_k^{LB}, the basic assumption is that all parcels $\sum_{i \in \mathcal{I}} l_i$ are combined in a single inbound truck and unloaded evenly over the complete standard time horizon T^{norm} as well as over all $|\mathcal{K}|$ conveyors. The lower limit r_k^{LB} is defined as follows:

$$r_k^{LB} = \frac{\sum_{i \in \mathcal{I}} l_i}{|\mathcal{K}| \cdot T^{norm}} \qquad (4.39)$$

As r_k^{LB} ignores the parcel allocation to individual inbound trucks, it constitutes a lower limit for the required conveyor capacity. The parameter $\sigma \geq 0$ defines the conveyor scarcity and increases or decreases the required conveyor capacity according to the scarcity level.

$$r_k = \lceil r_k^{LB} \cdot \sigma \rceil \tag{4.40}$$

Figure 4.14 illustrates the influence of the scarcity factor conveyor σ for an example with different levels of scarcity.

If the scarcity parameters σ is set to a value lower than one, the available resources are below the lower limit for the referenced planning horizon T^{norm}. Thus, the capacity is certainly not sufficient and tardy parcels are inevitable. Accordingly, if the conveyor scarcity parameter σ is greater than 1, a solution where all parcels reach their destinations before the deadline is theoretically possible. However, the conveyor scarcity factor σ does only relate to the conveyor capacity. Other resources such as the gate capacity might also constitute the bottleneck of the system. It also does not consider the parcel composition of the individual inbound trucks which can lead to further restrictions with regard to which inbound trucks can be unloaded concurrently. As a consequence, the optimal solution for most instances generated with $\sigma \geq 1$ still includes delayed parcels.

The same idea of an evenly distributed unloading process over the whole standard planning horizon T^{norm} is applied to compute the minimal number of gates U^{LB} with the following formula:

$$U^{LB} = \frac{\sum_{i \in \mathcal{I}} d_i}{T^{norm}} \tag{4.41}$$

Using the gate scarcity factor $\beta \geq 0$, we can compute the number of gates of an instance:

$$U = \lceil U^{LB} \cdot \beta \rceil \tag{4.42}$$

Figures 4.15, 4.16 and 4.17 show the resulting levels of gate capacity scarcity for different values of β.

We can again observe that if β is set to a value lower than 1, tardy parcels are inevitable since even for an idealized processing of the trucks the gate capacity would not suffice for a standard planning horizon T^{norm}. Accordingly, if $\beta \geq 1$ then all parcels are potentially unloaded before its respective deadline.

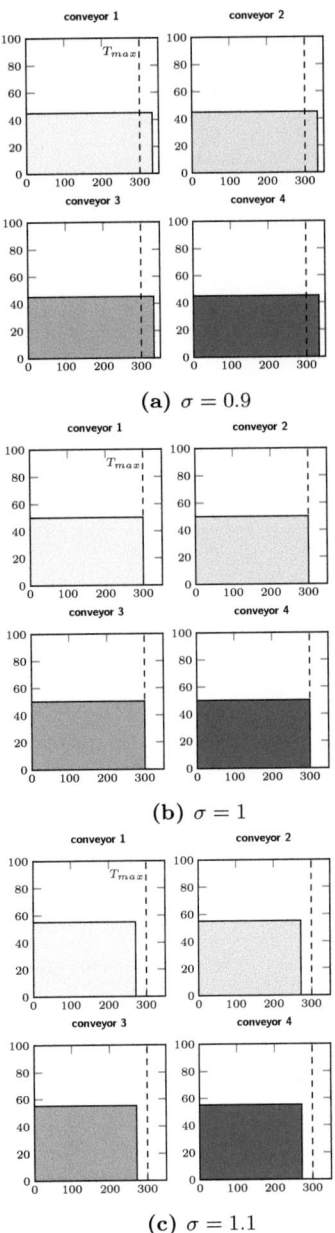

Figure 4.14.: Equalized conveyor capacity usage for different levels of scarcity

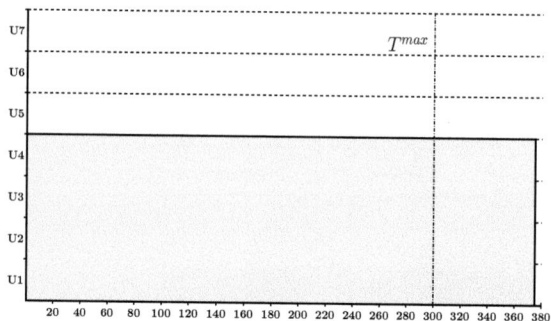

Figure 4.15.: Equalized gate capacity usage for $\beta = 0.8$

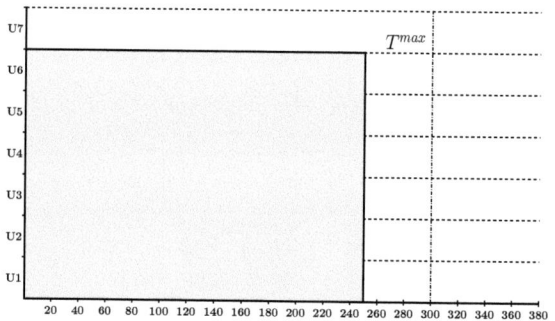

Figure 4.16.: Equalized gate capacity usage for $\beta = 1.2$

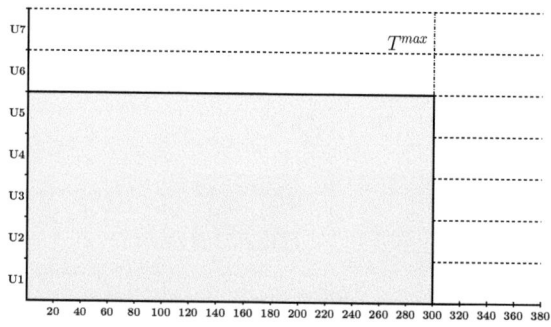

Figure 4.17.: Equalized gate capacity usage for $\beta = 1$

Experimental setup of the numerical study

Table 4.6 shows the fixed parameter values of the instances used in the numerical study. Each combination of the given parameters and class hub size receives five test instances generated with different random seeds. Thus, the total number of instances for both hub sizes is $2 \cdot 3^4 \cdot 5 = 810$. The instances are solved using the Python API of the standard solver

Table 4.6.: Instance data

Parameter	Small	Large
Inbound trucks $|\mathcal{I}|$	19	36
Outbound destinations $|\mathcal{O}|$	27	55
Conveyor belts $|\mathcal{K}|$	4	5
Parcels in inbound trucks l_i	650	
Standard length planning horizon T^{norm}	36	
Unloading duration d_i	10	
Parcel heterogeneity factor α	{0.4,0.6,0.8}	
Deadline time window factor μ	{0.1,0.2,0.3}	
Conveyor scarcity factor σ	{0.9,1,1.1}	
Gate scarcity factor β	{0.9,1,1.1}	

Gurobi 9.1. All computations are performed on the computer cluster of Leibniz University Hannover with a 2.93 GHz Intel Westmere-EP Xeon X5670 processor and 48 gigabytes of RAM.

The numerical study seeks to address two main points. First, the performance of the interval-based and time-based formulations of both the PHSP-LCC-fix and PHSP-LCC-flex are compared to empirically ascertain how hard the problem is to solve for the standard solver Gurobi. It also determines which formulation performs better with regard to the needed computational effort. Secondly, the potentials of controllable unloading speeds are investigated by comparing the results of the PHSP-LCC-fix and PHSP-LCC-flex for the given test sets. For both investigations, the influence of the instance parameters with a focus on the scarcity of the conveyor capacity and gates as well as the heterogeinity of parcel destinations and distribution of deadlines is included as well.

4.5.2. Results of the numerical study

Performance and comparison of the interval-based and time-based formulation

Table 4.7 depicts the numeric results for the PHSP-LCC-fix when applied to the instances corresponding to smaller and larger hubs. The results are presented with regard to the averages for the best found share of non-delayed parcels (*"on time"*), the remaining relative optimality gap in case the time limit of 3600 seconds is reached (*"gap"*), the number of instances solved to optimality (*"#"*) and the computation time (*"time"*) in seconds. Each line represents the results for the instances with a given combination of the parameters β and σ and thus 45 instances each.

Table 4.7.: Numerical results for the PHSP-LCC-fix

size	σ	β	time-based				interval-based			
			on time in %	gap in %	# opt	time in s	on time in %	gap in %	# opt	time in s
	0.9	0.9	76.44	0.0	45	5.51	76.44	0.0	45	5.7
	1.0	0.9	88.65	0.2	42	319.12	88.64	0.21	42	319.01
	1.1	0.9	90.92	0.0	45	0.38	90.92	0.0	45	0.25
	0.9	1.0	76.64	0.0	45	5.06	76.65	0.0	45	4.4
small	1.0	1.0	89.22	0.06	44	205.59	89.22	0.04	44	146.12
	1.1	1.0	91.14	0.02	44	83.54	91.14	0.0	45	3.42
	0.9	1.1	76.35	0.0	45	5.09	76.36	0.0	45	5.38
	1.0	1.1	89.11	0.05	43	187.39	89.11	0.04	43	176.98
	1.1	1.1	91.04	0.0	45	3.96	91.04	0.0	45	3.38
$\varnothing$			**85.5**	**0.04**	**44.22**	**90.63**	**85.5**	**0.03**	**44.33**	**73.85**
	0.9	0.9	79.97	6.91	0	3600	79.95	7.31	0	3600
	1.0	0.9	89.06	0.0	45	0.92	89.06	0.0	45	1.27
	1.1	0.9	88.95	0.0	45	0.38	88.95	0.0	45	0.23
	0.9	1.0	80.03	7.1	0	3600	79.96	7.65	0	3600
large	1.0	1.0	88.77	2.51	0	3600	88.82	2.84	0	3600
	1.1	1.0	92.48	0.0	45	0.9	92.48	0.0	45	0.45
	0.9	1.1	79.93	6.78	0	3600	80.04	7.06	0	3600
	1.0	1.1	88.86	2.39	0	3600	88.90	2.82	0	3600
	1.1	1.1	94.77	0.1	38	979.28	94.78	0.10	39	932.64
$\varnothing$			**86.98**	**2.87**	**19.22**	**2109.12**	**86.99**	**3.09**	**19.33**	**2103.87**

The results show that solving the instances using Gurobi for both model formulations leads to similar results. The smaller instances are generally easier to solve as only 7 instances could not be solved to optimality for the time-based formulation and 6 for the interval-based formulation. The average computation time is also rather short with 90.63 seconds for the time-based formulation and 73.85 seconds for the interval-based formulation on average. The average computation time is calculated using all instances, including those that could not be solved to optimality. The remaining optimality gap is very low for the interval-based formulation as all instances show a gap of less than 1 % in case they were not solved to optimality. The larger instances are harder to solve for Gurobi. For the time-based formulation only 173 out of 405 instances and for the interval-based formulation 174 instances were solved to optimality within the time limit. Remarkably, we can observe two distinct categories of instances in the results when considering specific combination of the parameters β and σ. The first category only consists of instances with an average gap close to zero, for example for $\beta = 0.9$ and $\sigma = 1.0$ whereas the second category, such as $\beta = 0.9$ and $\sigma = 0.9$, only includes instances that could not be solved to optimality. To further investigate the influence of instance parameters on the performance of the model formulations refer to Figure 4.18.

Figure 4.18 shows the average computation time of both model formulations to solve instances with specific values for the parcel destination heterogeneity factor α, the deadline distribution μ, conveyor scarcity σ and gate scarcity β. Each bar thus reflects 135 instances.

As the smaller instances are comparatively easy to solve, we also only observe minor differences with regard to the computation time. However, it is notable that instances with a conveyor scarcity of $\sigma = 1$ seem to be harder to solve. Instances with a lower parcel destination heterogeneity α lead to results with higher computation time than those with low levels of parcel heterogeneity.

For the larger instances, we can observe a strong correlation of the computational time with both the conveyor scarcity σ as well as the gate scarcity β. For those instances with very scarce conveyor capacities and thus $\sigma = 0.9$, the optimal solution could not be found for any instance resulting in an average computation time of 3600 seconds. In contrast, most instances for $\sigma = 1.1$ were solved to optimality with average computation times of 328 and 313 seconds, respectively. Concerning gate scarcity, instances with low values of β appear to be easier to solve. For low values of β the gates constitute the bottleneck of the system more often and are thus comparable to those with a high value of the conveyor scarcity factor $\sigma = 1.1$. This indicates that scarce conveyor capacities have the strongest impact on how hard it is to solve an instance. Further, parcel destination heterogeneity and the deadline time window do not seem to influence the performance of both model formulations utilizing

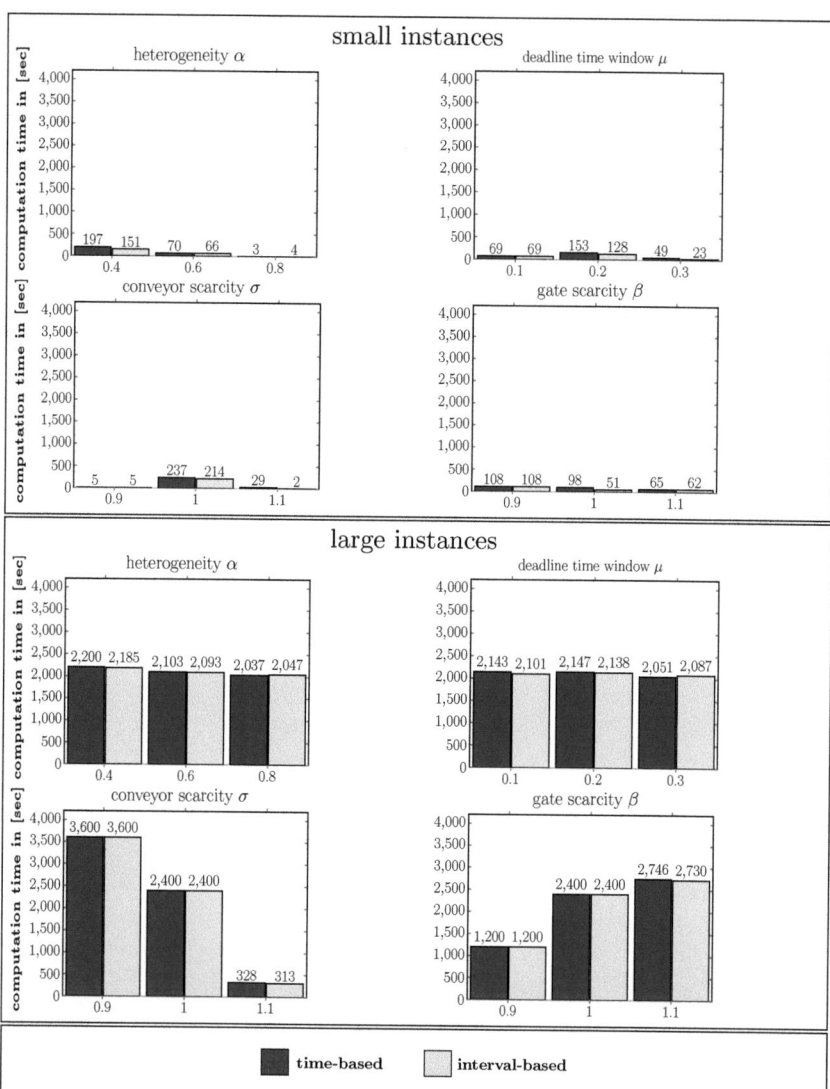

Figure 4.18.: Influence of instance parameters on the computational time of interval-based and time-based formulations for the PHSP-LCC-fix

Gurobi as the resulting computation times for all values of α and μ only show minor deviations from each other. Table 4.8 shows the numeric results for the PHSP-LCC-flex.

Table 4.8.: Numerical results for the PHSP-LCC-flex

size	σ	β	time-based				interval-based			
			on time in %	gap in %	#	time in s	on time in %	gap in %	#	time in s
	0.9	0.9	85.11	7.04	2	3481.94	85.29	0.65	6	3344.79
	1.0	0.9	89.75	16.06	0	3600	90.14	0.07	35	1402.01
	1.1	0.9	90.87	20.71	0	3600	91.03	0.0	45	179.23
	0.9	1.0	86.59	1.21	9	3033.20	86.59	0.16	18	2613.37
small	1.0	1.0	91.86	2.33	6	3317.04	91.92	0.04	32	1730.75
	1.1	1.0	95.71	18.93	2	3463.91	95.81	0.01	44	906.11
	0.9	1.1	86.28	0.12	33	1740.69	86.28	0.02	33	1396.09
	1.0	1.1	92.08	0.40	33	1665.36	92.08	0.01	42	800.04
	1.1	1.1	95.71	0.11	35	1421.03	95.71	0.01	44	353.15
∅			**90.44**	**7.43**	**13.33**	**2813.7**	**90.54**	**0.11**	**33.22**	**1413.95**
	0.9	0.9	85.33	13.44	0	3600	86.40	0.62	0	3600
	1.0	0.9	88.19	10.24	0	3600	89.16	0.0	45	276.84
	1.1	0.9	88.48	5.75	0	3600	88.95	0.0	45	71.31
	0.9	1.0	86.97	5.34	0	3600	87.08	0.46	3	3437.44
large	1.0	1.0	91.37	23.6	0	3600	90.10	0.37	14	3077.86
	1.1	1.0	92.15	37.62	0	3600	92.49	0.01	45	486.98
	0.9	1.1	87.17	1.03	3	3508.92	87.18	0.07	16	2903.08
	1.0	1.1	93.20	2.54	2	3539.18	93.27	0.03	26	2606.38
	1.1	1.1	97.26	5.19	0	3600	97.33	0.01	34	1599.89
∅			**90.01**	**11.64**	**0.56**	**3583.12**	**90.22**	**0.17**	**25.33**	**2006.66**

Contrary to the PHSP-LCC-fix, the time-based and interval-based formulations for the PHSP-LCC-flex perform substantially different. The time-based formulation generally terminates with a higher average gap and computation time for all instances and can only solve 120 of the smaller instances and 5 of the larger instances to optimality. The interval-based formulation on the other hand solves 258 of the smaller instances and 225 of the larger instances to optimality. Thus, applying the interval-based formulation seems generally beneficial in this case. Figure 4.19 shows the average computation time of both model formulations to solve instances with specific values of the considered instance parameters for the PHSP-LCC-flex. For both the smaller and larger instances, higher values of the conveyor scarcity factor σ again lead to significantly shorter computation times for the interval-based formulation. Further, instances with high parcel destination heterogeneity α and smaller deadline time windows μ also seem slightly easier to be solved for the interval-based formulation. With regard to the time-based formulation, we can only state that solving instances with lower gate scarcity β seems to be easier. Most instances are, however, not solved to optimality and consequentially all reach the time limit. Compared to the PHSP-LCC-fix, the instance size appears to have a smaller impact on the performance of the formulations as the computation time deviates less between the instance sizes.

The numeric study shows empirically that attaining an optimal solution with a standard solver for both formulations of the PHSP-LCC-fix and PHSP-LCC-flex can require a substantial amount of time. Considering an operational planning setting, truck schedules should be generated quickly. Thus, a fast heuristic approach for solving the problem is presented in Chapter 5.

Assessing the potentials of controllable unloading speeds

As the second part of the numeric analysis, the potentials of using controllable unloading speeds are explored by comparing the results of the PHSP-LCC-fix and PHSP-LCC-flex. The results shown in Figures 4.7 and 4.8 constitute the basis for the comparison of both models. To assess the potentials of flexible unloading speeds, we compare the share of non-delayed parcels for the optimal solution of the PHSP-LCC-fix and PHSP-LCC-flex for each instance. Figure 4.20 shows the increase of the share of non-delayed parcels for different levels of destination heterogeneity α, deadline time windows μ, conveyor scarcity σ and gate scarcity β for both classes of instances. Each bar represents the average relative increase of the number of parcels arriving on time for all instances with the stated value of the parameters α, μ, σ and β and includes 135 instances each.

We can observe that assuming flexible unloading speeds leads to an increase of the share of parcels without delay for all instances. Since the PHSP-LCC-flex can be seen as a generalization of the PHSP-LCC-fix as shown in Section 4.4 on page 64, these results were to be expected. Generally, the share of non-delayed parcels can be increased by 5.67 % on average for the smaller instances and by 3.82 % on average for the larger instances. We do, however, see significant divergences of the potentials of controllable unloading speeds considering instances with specific parameters. Here, especially the results for small values of σ and thus scarce capacities stand out as the share of parcels without delay increases by an average of 10.93 % for the small instances and 7.79 % for the large instances under the assumption of flexible unloading speeds, re-

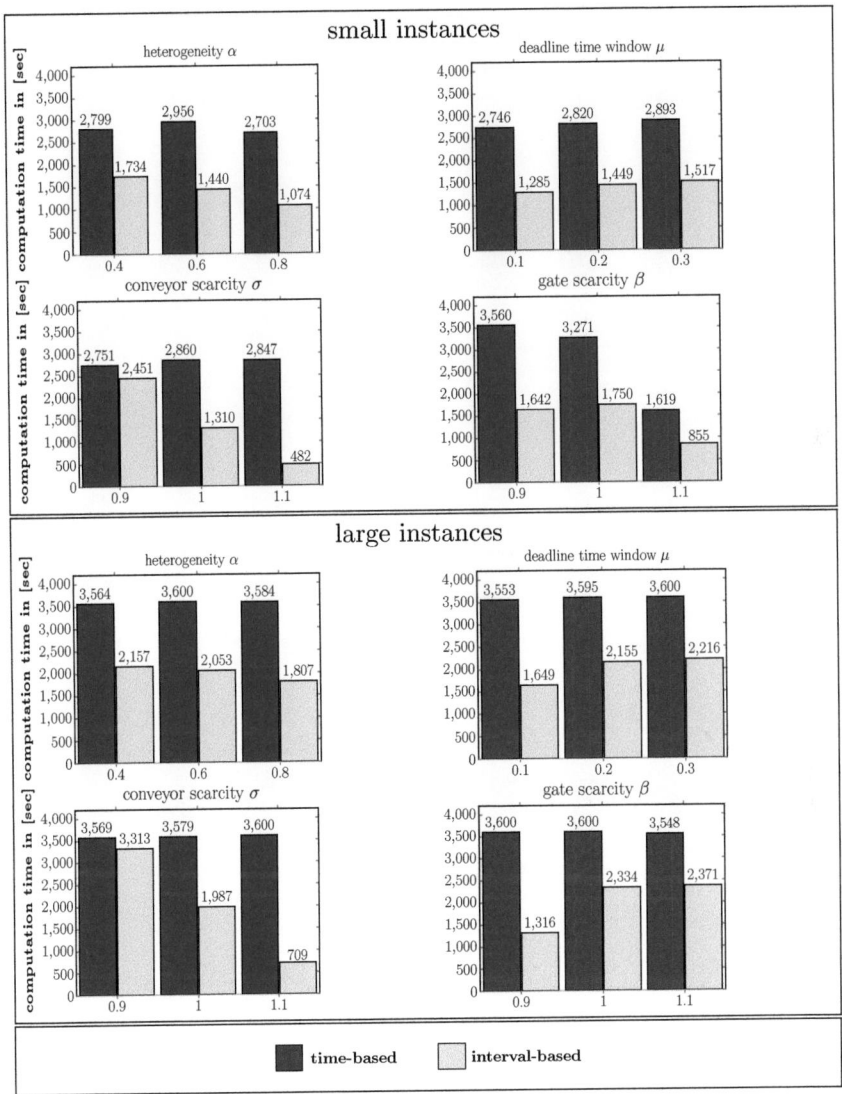

Figure 4.19.: Influence of instance parameters on the computational time of interval-based and time-based formulations for the PHSP-LCC-flex

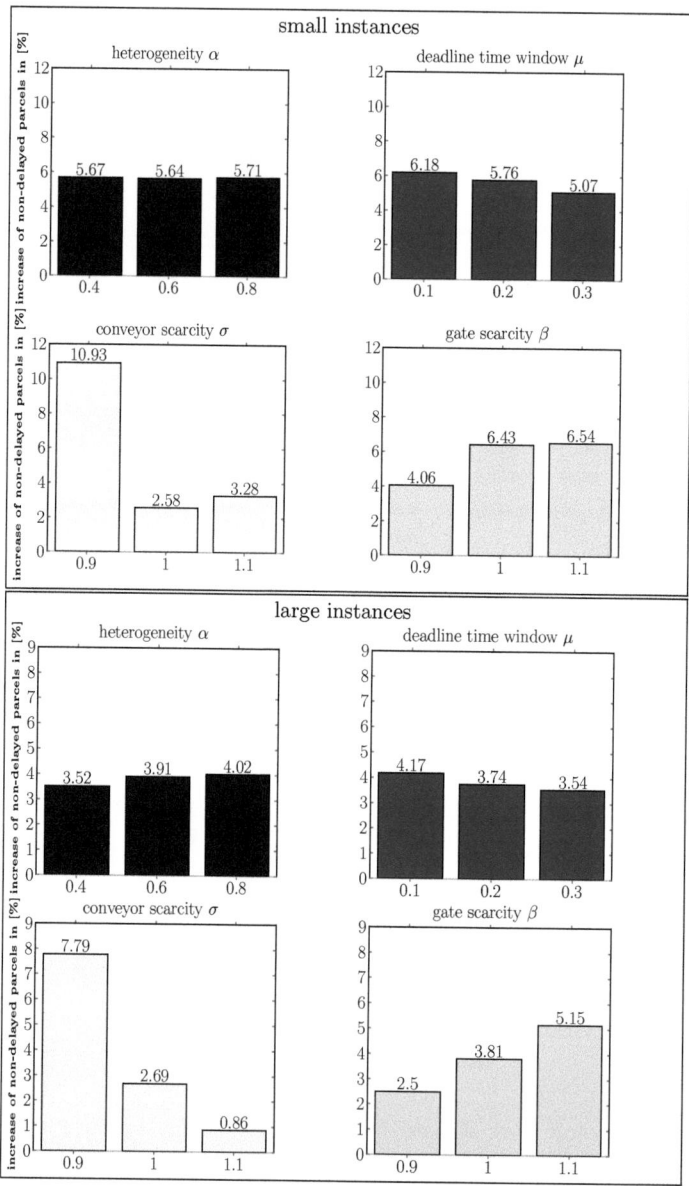

Figure 4.20.: Comparison of the PHSP-LCC-fix and PHSP-LCC-flex

spectively. These instances represent hubs with especially scarce conveyor capacities. Since the average increase of parcels without delay for higher values of σ is much smaller, the results confirm that assuming flexible unloading speeds is only a promising approach for operational settings where the conveyors actually constitute the bottleneck of the system. The importance of the conveyor capacity as bottleneck for the performance of controllable unloading speeds is also observable with regard to the results for different levels of gate scarcity β. Here, a higher number of gates leads to a larger increase of the share of non-delayed parcels since the conveyors are more likely to be the bottleneck of the system in these cases.

Regarding the remaining instance parameters, the parcel destination heterogeneity α seems to have little impact on the potential of flexible unloading speeds as we receive similar results for each value of α and both instance sizes. Similarly, the deadline time window μ also only has a minor influence on the potentials of flexible unloading speeds.

In conclusion, the numeric study shows that increasing flexibility in the unloading process by controlling unloading speeds is especially valuable in operational settings with scarce conveyor capacities. If the gates constitute the bottleneck of the system, however, the potentials of controllable unloading speeds diminish.

5. Heuristic solution of the PHSP-LCC-flex with a genetic algorithm

5.1. Motivation and overview of heuristic solution methods for the truck scheduling problem at cross docks

The truck scheduling problem at cross docks for different applications has been widely studied in literature as shown in Chapter 3. To solve the problem in its various forms, different solution methods have been developed. For an overview of approaches refer to Van Belle et al. (2012), Ladier and Alpan (2016a) and Theophilus et al. (2019). We can differentiate between exact and heuristic solution methods. Exact solution methods can provide proven optimal solutions but usually require high computational effort. Heuristic solutions aim at generating good solutions in short order but these solutions are not necessarily optimal.[1] As the truck scheduling problem is an operational planning problem, finding a good solution in a short time frame is often of high importance. Since the problem is NP-hard, finding a proven optimal solution with exact methods is often too time-consuming in most relevant configurations. Thus, heuristic approaches enjoy great popularity in literature[2] since they generate adequate solutions comparably fast, even for larger instances. Heuristic solution approaches range from specially tailored dedicated heuristics and LP-based heuristics to metaheuristic approaches such as tabu search, simulated annealing, particle swarm and others.[3] Here, especially genetic algorithms are frequently used. Thus, a genetic

---

[1] Zanakis and Evans (1981, p. 84).
[2] Theophilus et al. (2019, p. 17).
[3] Ladier and Alpan (2016a, p. 150).

algorithm is developed to solve the PHSP-LCC-flex heuristically. The genetic algorithm has already been illustrated in Bugow and Kellenbrink (2023).

5.2. A genetic algorithm for the PHSP-LCC-flex

5.2.1. General structure of genetic algorithms

Genetic algorithms are metaheuristic algorithms inspired by the basic principle of natural selection as formulated by Darwin (1859) and Mendel (1866) and belong to the wider class of evolutionary algorithms.[4] Meta-heuristic algorithms, such as genetic algorithms, are usually employed for dealing with optimization problems that are hard to solve, especially if these problems are NP-hard.[5] They provide a general purpose framework that can be applied to different types of optimization problems and search the solution space in phases of exploration and exploitation.[6] Genetic algorithms use a population of solutions (individuals) that are represented according to their *genotype* and evaluated according to their *phenotype*. Here, the *genotype* constitutes the encoded representation of a solution and the *phenotype* is the corresponding actual solution of the problem.[7] The solutions are subjected to variations by genetic operators over multiple iterations. Iterations are also frequently referred to as *generations*. Relevant types of genetic operators are recombination and mutation. Recombination operators combine two individuals to generate new individuals whereas mutation operators alter individuals. In each generation a specified number of individuals is selected to stay for the next generation and the remaining individuals are discarded. Usually, the selected individuals are predominantly of high quality. Thus, the selection process ensures that the whole population is drifting towards promising sections of the solution space and avoids remaining in local optima through the usage of a population of solutions.[8] The basic structure of a genetic algorithm is shown in Algorithm 5.1

---

[4]Holland (1975).
[5]Yang (2010, p. 8).
[6]Rothlauf (2011, pp. 147-148).
[7]Glover and Kochenberger (2006, p. 57).
[8]Rothlauf (2011, p. 149).

Algorithm 5.1: Basic genetic algorithm

Input: Instance of the problem
Output: Solution
1 create initial population and corresponding fitness values
2 **while** *stopping criterion not met* **do**
3 | select and recombine parents to create new offspring
4 | mutate offspring
5 | calculate fitness of offspring
6 | select individuals for the next generation
7 return individual with best fitness

The algorithms starts with generating an initial population and is executed until the stated termination criterion is met. Frequently used termination criteria are a specified number of generations, an upper limit of evaluations of the fitness function or when the probability of finding a better solution in a following generation is low.[9]

In each generation, pairs of individuals are selected for reproduction and recombined to generate a new individual. The pairs of selected individuals are often designated as *parents* and the newly generated individuals as *offspring*. We can apply different methods for selecting individuals for reproduction. An exemplary method is fitness-proportionate selection where individuals with higher quality are more likely to be selected.[10] Offspring are then subjected to the mutation operator and their fitness is calculated. The fitness constitutes the measurement of the individual's quality. At the end of each generation, the extended population of parents and offspring is reduced to the standard population size by selecting the remaining individuals for the following generation according to the selection method. An exemplary method would be elitist selection that only selects the fittest individuals for the next generation.[11] The individual with the highest fitness in the last generation is the solution of the genetic algorithm.

As a metaheuristic optimization method, genetic algorithms constitute a problem-independent basic framework. To apply the algorithm to specific problems, finding a suitable solution representation for the algorithm to operate on is usually the first step. With a suitable representation, we can then define problem-specific genetic operators for recombination

---

[9]Safe et al. (2004, p. 406).
[10]Tomassini (1995, p. 96).
[11]Thierens and D. Goldberg (1994, p. 508).

i	$i1$	$i2$	$i3$	$i4$	$i5$	$i6$
$door$	1	2	1	1	2	2

Figure 5.1.: Exemplary gate-based representation

and mutation. Further, methods for generating a starting population and for calculating the fitness of a solution have to be specified as well. Lastly, the problem-independent components of the algorithm such as population size and termination criterion have to be adjusted for the specific problem.[12]

5.2.2. Overview of genetic algorithms for the truck scheduling problem at cross docks

As a first step to implement a genetic algorithm for any specific variant of the problem, we have to define an adequate representation of the solutions. If the representation is chosen inadequately, it can negatively influence the search procedure and efficiency of the algorithm.[13] In the following, genetic algorithms for the truck scheduling problem at cross docks are classified according to their representation. Generally, representations for truck scheduling problems at cross docks can be subdivided into three distinct categories: solely based on gate assignment, based on combined gate assignment and truck sequencing or permutation-based. For those variants of the truck scheduling problem where inbound trucks $i \in \mathcal{I}$ are assigned to specific doors, one approach is to represent solutions based on gate assignment by encode them as a vector. Each entry of the vector references one inbound truck i and specifies inbound door i is assigned to. Figure 5.1 shows an exemplary solution for an instance with two inbound doors and six inbound trucks encoded according to the gate-based representation.

In the example, inbound trucks i1, i3 and i4 would be assigned to the first gate whereas i2, i5 and i6 would be assigned to the second gate. Genetic algorithms using this representation can be found in Bermudez et al. (2001), Lim et al. (2006), V. F. Yu et al. (2008) and Bjelić et al. (2013).

---

[12]Koza (1995, p. 589).
[13]McWilliams et al. (2005, p. 404).

i	$i1$	$i2$	$i3$	$i4$	$i5$	$i6$
door	1	2	1	1	2	2
seq	1	2	3	2	3	1

Figure 5.2.: Exemplary representation combining gate assignment and truck sequencing

The gate-based representation does not specify the sequence of inbound trucks at the inbound doors and is mostly used for the dock-door assignment problem and problem settings where the sequence of the trucks at the gates is not relevant. Other approaches include the precedence relations of inbound trucks at the doors by separating the inbound truck sequences at the individual doors from each other. Figure 5.2 illustrates an exemplary solution for the given instance with six inbound trucks and two gates.

The inbound trucks receive the same gate assignment as in Figure 5.1 with inbound trucks i1, i3 and i4 assigned to the first gate and i2, i5 and i6 assigned to the second gate. Using the second row of the representation, we can now also identify the sequence of the inbound trucks. At the first gate, i1 is unloaded before i4 and i3 whereas i6 is unloaded before i2 and i5 at the second gate. The representation is used by Molavi et al. (2018) to solve a truck scheduling problem with fixed due dates. The concept of explicitly expressing gate assignment and truck scheduling together in the representation can also be found in Ley and Elfayoumy (2007), Davoudpour et al. (2012), Golias et al. (2012) and Konur and Golias (2013).

The third and final category of representations for the truck scheduling problem is the permutation-based representation. Here, a solution is defined as a vector of inbound trucks and we generate the corresponding truck schedule by sequencing the inbound trucks according to the order they appear in the vector. The representation is mainly used in settings where inbound gates are aggregated to a single gate or when the specific assignment of inbound trucks to doors is irrelevant and only a combined sequence of inbound trucks is required. Refer to Vahdani and Zandieh (2010), Shiguemoto et al. (2014) and Guo et al. (2012) for applications of genetic algorithms with this representation. An example of the permutation-based representation is given in Figure 5.3.

i	$i2$	$i4$	$i1$	$i5$	$i3$	$i6$

Figure 5.3.: Exemplary permutation-based representation

U2	i4	i5	i6
U1	i2	i1	i3

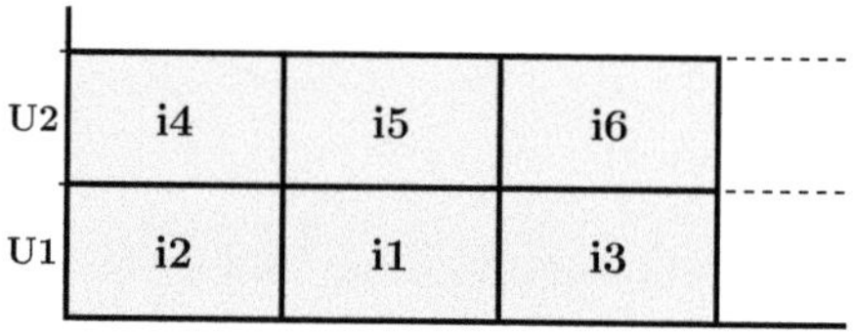

Figure 5.4.: Exemplary schedule for the permutation-based representation

In the example, i2 is scheduled first followed by i4, i1, i5, i3 and finally i6. The permutation-based representation can also be used for problem settings where an explicit gate assignment is required through the introduction of a dispatching rule. A dispatching rule is a procedure to generate a feasible truck schedule by assigning inbound trucks to inbound doors using the sequence of inbound trucks specified in the representation. Dispatching rules bear similarities to schedule generation schemes for the resource-constrained project scheduling problem that generate feasible schedules from a given priority list of activities for the problem.[14]
An exemplary dispatching rule would be to iteratively assign inbound trucks to the door with the earliest ending time of the currently assigned inbound trucks. If we assume that all inbound trucks have the same unloading time, applying the stated dispatching rule to the example form Figure 5.3 yields the truck schedule given in Figure 5.4.

Genetic algorithms using a permutation-based representation in conjunction with dispatching rules have been studied by McWilliams et al. (2005), McWilliams (2009b) and Joo and Kim (2013). The remainder of the chapter is dedicated to illustrating a genetic algorithm with a random-key representation of the solution for the PHSP-LCC-flex that employs a dispatching rule specially tailored to the PHSP-LCC-flex. The random-key representation is closely connected to the permutation-based encoding of solutions but uses a vector of random numbers as a basis to generate a truck sequence.

---

[14]Kolisch (1996, p. 322).

5.2.3. Representation of the solution for the PHSP-LCC-flex

Random-key representation of the solution

The random-key representation encodes a solution as a string of random real numbers, usually taken from the range between 0 and 1. The random keys of a solution are utilized to first generate a sequence of the jobs or trucks by sorting them according to the random keys. This sequence is then employed to devise a feasible schedule according to a decoding scheme. Throughout the execution of the genetic algorithm, the algorithm finds connections between the objective function values and random keys and exploits these to find solutions with high fitness.[15] The advantage of a random-key representation is that every solution encoded as random keys and all offspring generated by the genetic operators are always feasible. Thus, additional computational effort for repair procedures of infeasible solutions can be avoided.[16] Genetic algorithms with a random-key representation have been successfully applied to a variety of optimization problems and especially scheduling problems.[17] With regard to genetic algorithms for truck scheduling problems at cross docks, Liao et al. (2014) and Yazdani et al. (2015) propose an algorithm based on random keys for a multi-dock cross dock and Vahdani and Zandieh (2010) use the concept for a problem setting with explicit consideration of temporary storage.

For the PHSP-LCC-flex, a solution is represented as a string of I real values between 0 and 1 defining their priority. Thus, each inbound i receives a priority value. The random-key encoded representation of the solution is first decoded to a sequence of inbound trucks according to their priority. The resulting sequence matches the permutation-based representation of solutions illustrated in Section 5.2.2. Lastly, the actual solution or its phenotype is determined using a dispatching rule that generates a feasible truck schedule for the PHSP-LCC-flex. The values of the individual random keys are mostly arbitrary in the first generations of the genetic algorithm but converged to values that constitute truck schedules with high fitness. Figure 5.5 shows how an exemplary solution λ in random-key representation is decoded into a sequence of inbound trucks.

---

[15]Mendes et al. (2009, p. 96).
[16]Bean (1994, p. 157).
[17]Prasetyo et al. (2015, p. 863).

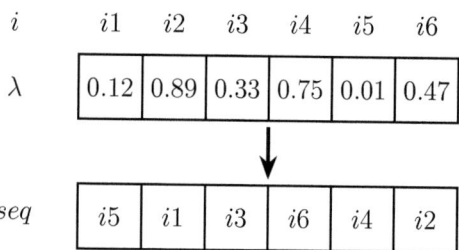

Figure 5.5.: Exemplary solution in random-key representation

In the given example, we sort the inbound trucks according to the value of their corresponding random key, starting with the smallest value. In this case, inbound i5 is scheduled first and followed by i1, i3, i6, i4 and lastly i2. The sequence is then used as an input for the dispatching rule to generate the phenotype of the solution. The dispatching rule is illustrated in the following section.

Decoding scheme for solutions in random-key representation

To implement an adequate decoding scheme for the PHSP-LCC-flex, we have to consider the distinctive features of the problem. Since each encoded solution should constitute a feasible solution for the original problem, the decoded solution must also adhere to the restrictions regarding the gate and conveyor capacity. Further, we should be able to utilize the flexibility offered through controllable unloading speeds. The result of the decoding procedure should be a feasible truck schedule that provides starting and ending times for each inbound as well as the number of unloaded parcels in each period. On the basis of the generated schedule, the fitness of the solution can be calculated.

The basic approach for the dispatching rule is to schedule the inbound trucks in order of the sequence given by the representation. Each inbound truck is assigned to an inbound door and then unloads as many parcels as possible in the following periods until the inbound truck is empty. Algorithm 5.2 illustrates the decoding procedure.

Algorithm 5.2: Decoding procedure for a solution of the PHSP-LCC-flex in random-key representation

---

Input: Instance
$$P = (\mathcal{I}, \mathcal{O}, \mathcal{K}, \mathcal{T}, U, r_k, x_i^{max}, l_i, lk_{ik}, dl_o, ship_{io}, at_i)$$
Solution in random-key notation

Output: Feasible truck schedule

1 initialize earliest possible starting time at gates to
  $ES_u := 0 \ \forall u \in \mathcal{G}$
2 initialize conveyor utilization to $rt_{kt} := 0 \ \forall k \in \mathcal{K}, t \in \mathcal{T}$
3 initialize unloading status $load_i := l_i \ \forall i \in \mathcal{I}$
4 initialize unloading status $x_{it}^{share} := 0 \ \forall i \in \mathcal{I}, t \in \mathcal{T}$
5 decode random-key encoded solution λ^{RK} into inbound truck
  sequence seq
6 set current period $t^c := 1$
7 **for** $i \in seq$ **do**
8   select gate u' with earliest possible starting time $ES_{u'}$
9      $t^c = \max(at_i, ES_{u'})$
10      $z_i^{start} = t^c$
11   **while** $load_i > 0$ **do**
12   calculate maximum share of unloaded parcels
   $$x_{it^c}^{share} = \min(\min_{k \in \mathcal{K}}(\tfrac{r_k - rt_{kt^c}}{lk_{ik}}), \tfrac{x_i^{max}}{l_i}, \tfrac{load_i}{l_i})$$
13          $rt_{kt^c} = rt_{kt^c} + x_{it^c}^{share} \cdot lk_{ik} \ \forall k \in \mathcal{K}$
14          $load_i = load_i - x_{it^c}^{share} \cdot l_i$
15   **if** $load_i = 0$ **then**
16             $z_i^{end} = t^c$
17             $ES_{u'} = t^c$
18   **else**
19             $t^c = t^c + 1$

As a first step, we initialize earliest starting times ES_u at the gates $u \in \mathcal{G}$, the gate utilization rt_{kt} in each period t and the initial unloading status $load_i$ of all inbound trucks i. Further, the share of unloaded parcels in each period x_{it}^{share} is initialized. The inbound trucks are sorted according to their random keys λ^{RK} and transformed into the sequence seq. Afterwards, the scheduling procedure for each inbound truck starts by first determining the inbound gate with the earliest possible starting time. The current time period t^c is then set to either the arrival time at_i of the current inbound truck or the earliest starting time $ES_{u'}$ at gate u', whichever is larger. Here, gate u' refers to the gate with the earliest starting times out of all the gates. If several gates have the same earliest starting time, a gate is chosen according to the smallest index rule. This way, each inbound is scheduled as early as possible. The unloading process starts with determining the starting time z_i^{start} of inbound i. Generally, we calculate the maximum share of parcels that can leave the inbound truck in each period until the inbound truck is empty. Here, the maximum share x_{it}^{share} of unloaded parcels is either limited by the remaining conveyor capacity $\frac{r_k - rt_{ktc}}{lk_{ik}}$, the maximum unloading speed $\frac{x_i^{max}}{l_i}$ or the remaining parcels in the inbound truck $\frac{load_i}{l_i}$. The maximum share of unloaded parcels is then employed to update the conveyor utilization in the current period rt_{kt} and the remaining number of parcels in the inbound truck $load_i$. We repeat the procedure until $load_i = 0$ and thus no parcels remain in the inbound truck. Once the truck is empty, the ending time z_i^{end} is set to the current period and we update the earliest possible starting time $ES_{u'}$ of gate u' to the following period. Once all inbound trucks included in the sequence λ^{RK} are unloaded, the algorithm terminates. Accordingly, we only assign inbound trucks to U distinct gates once the preceding truck has been fully unloaded and account for the conveyor capacity when calculating the maximum share of unloaded parcels. Thus, the procedure always generates a feasible, but not necessarily optimal, truck schedule for the given sequence. The fitness of the resulting truck schedule is calculated as follows:

$$f(\lambda^{RK}) = \sum_{o \in \mathcal{O}} \sum_{t=1}^{dl_o} \sum_{i \in \mathcal{I}} x_{it}^{share} \cdot ship_{io} \qquad (5.1)$$

The formula closely resembles the objective function of the PHSP-LCC-flex as it also calculates number of non-delayed parcels.

To illustrate the decoding scheme, we apply it to a small example with 3 inbound trucks $i1, i2, i3$ 2 inbound gates $U1$ and $U2$ 1 outbound truck $o1$ and 1 conveyor $k1$. Each inbound truck has a maximum unloading speed of $x_i^{max} = 10$ parcels per time period and contains $l_i = 50$ parcels. Thus, the standard unloading duration is 5 time periods for each inbound truck.

The single conveyor $k1$ transports the parcels to the only outbound gate $o1$ and has a capacity of $r^{max} = 15$ parcels per period. The inbound trucks are scheduled according to the sequence $seq = \{i2, i3, i1\}$. The first iteration is shown in Figure 5.6.

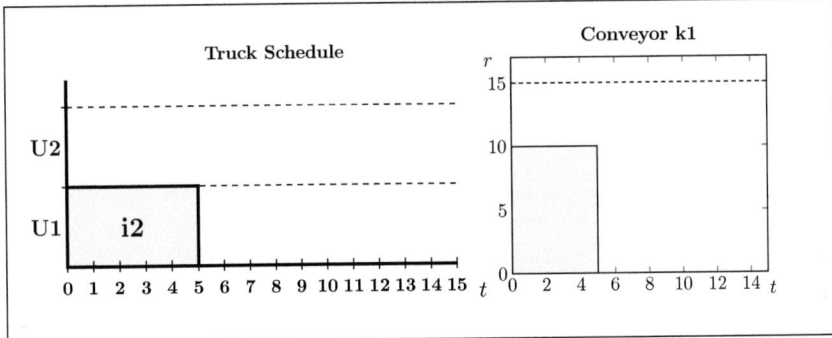

Figure 5.6.: Decoding scheme example: scheduling first truck

As all gates are unoccupied at the start of the procedure, the first truck is assigned to the first gate. The unloading process of the first truck is only limited by the maximum unloading speed as the conveyor capacity is not reached throughout its execution. Thus, 10 parcels are unloaded every period of its unloading process:

$$x_{it} = \min(r_{max} - rt_{tk}, x_i^{max}, load_i)$$
$$= \min\{15, 10, \{50, ..., 10\}\}$$
$$= 10$$

Note that for the purpose of a more intuitive illustration the *number* of unloaded parcels rather than the *share* of unloaded parcels is presented for the example. Figure 5.7 illustrates how inbound truck $i3$ is scheduled according to the decoding scheme. The second truck of the sequence $i3$ is assigned to the second gate $U2$ as the earliest possible starting time at $U2$ is the smallest of all available gates. The unloading process is limited to 5 parcels per period by the remaining conveyor capacity until period $t5$:

$$x_{it} = \min(r_{max} - rt_{tk}, x_i^{max}, load_i)$$
$$= \min\{5, 10, \{50, ..., 25\}\}$$
$$= 5$$

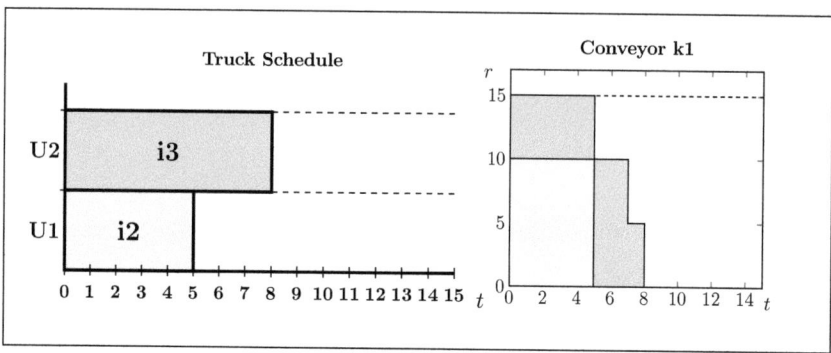

Figure 5.7.: Decoding scheme example: scheduling second truck

Afterwards, the maximum unloading speed is the limiting factor again and 10 parcels can be unloaded in the periods $t6$ and $t7$:

$$x_{it} = \min(r_{max} - rt_{tk}, x_i^{max}, load_i)$$
$$= \min\{15, \mathbf{10}, \{25, 15\}\}$$
$$= 10$$

As the truck is nearly fully unloaded in period $t8$, the remaining number of parcels inside in the inbound truck limits the unloading speed to 5 parcels:

$$x_{it} = \min(r_{max} - rt_{tk}, x_i^{max}, load_i)$$
$$= \min\{15, 10, \mathbf{5}\}$$
$$= 5$$

Lastly, Figure 5.8 shows the how the decoding procedure is applied to schedule the third inbound truck of the sequence $i1$. The third truck is assigned to the first gate again. The unloading speed of the third truck is first limited to 5 parcel per period by the remaining conveyor capacity in the periods $t5$ and $t7$:

$$x_{it} = \min(r_{max} - rt_{tk}, x_i^{max}, load_i)$$
$$= \min\{\mathbf{5}, 10, \{50, 45\}\}$$
$$= 5$$

For the remainder of its unloading process it can be unloaded with the maximum unloading speed of 10 parcels per period as it is neither limited

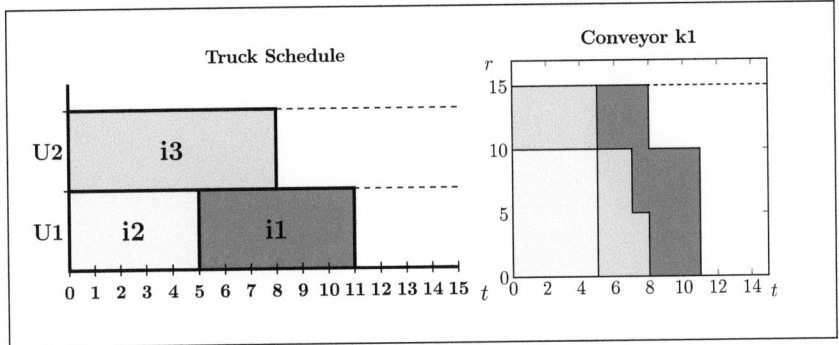

Figure 5.8.: Decoding scheme example: scheduling third truck

by the conveyor capacity nor the remaining number of parcels inside the truck:

$$x_{it} = \min(r_{max} - rt_{tk}, x_i^{max}, load_i)$$
$$= \min\{15, \mathbf{10}, \{40, 10\}\}$$
$$= 10$$

Considering the final truck schedule in Figure 5.8, we can observe that only inbound truck $i2$ is scheduled with its standard duration of 5 periods and $i3$ and $i1$ extend their unloading process to not exceed the conveyor capacity. Thus, the example shows how the decoding procedure aims to always fully utilize the conveyor capacity by controlling the unloading speed of the individual inbound trucks.

To further illustrate the results of the decoding procedure, we apply the method to the instance with 19 inbound trucks, 27 outbound trucks, 8 inbound gates and 4 conveyors considered in Chapter 4 on page 31. As an exemplary solution, we randomly generate a key for each truck. Using those keys, the decoding scheme is used to generate a solution. Figure 5.9 illustrates the resulting truck schedule and conveyor utilization. The truck schedule resulting from the decoding procedure results in $\sum_o U_o = 8281$ non-delayed parcels and a schedule length of $C_{max} = 250$. Some inbound trucks, such as i3, i4, i5 and i10, are unloaded with the standard unloading duration whereas all others prolong their unloading process and thus make use of controllable unloading speeds. Further, we can observe that at least one conveyor is always fully utilized in case all inbound gates are currently occupied. However, the remaining conveyors frequently operate

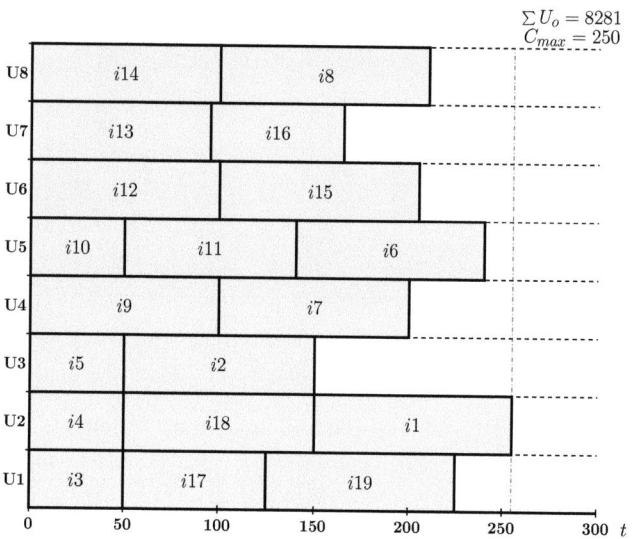

$$\Sigma U_o = 8281$$
$$C_{max} = 250$$

(a) Optimized schedule

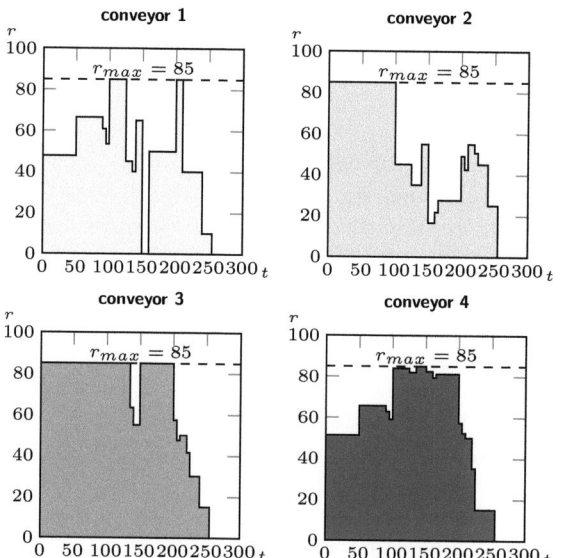

(b) Optimized conveyor utilization

Figure 5.9.: Truck schedule and conveyor utilization for an exemplary decoded solution

significantly below their capacity.

Generally, the procedure generates truck schedules in which inbound trucks start their unloading process as early as possible and utilize the conveyor capacity of the current bottleneck conveyor fully. However, the method comes with three main limitations.

(1) **Deadlines are not considered**

The objective of maximizing the number of non-delayed parcels is only considered implicitly by scheduling inbound trucks as early as possible. Since the respective deadlines of the inbound trucks are not taken into account as we decide on the number of unloaded parcels in each period, the total number of non-delayed parcels is oftentimes still suboptimal.

(2) **Unloading speed flexibility is limited**

Since the number of unloaded parcels in each period is determined for each inbound truck sequentially, only a single inbound truck receives a number of unloaded parcels that differs from either no parcels at all or the maximum number of parcels as set by the standard unloading speed. Thus, the flexibility offered by controllable unloading speeds is severely restricted.

(3) **Intended delays are disregarded**

Intended delays cannot be included with the approach of scheduling each inbound truck as early as possible and always unloading the maximum number of parcels. Thus, in circumstances where stopping the unloading process of one inbound truck to allow for a faster unloading process of other currently unloaded inbound trucks with tighter deadlines is not possible.

To summarize, the stated standard decoding procedure can potentially lead to comparably poor solutions as it excludes areas of the feasible space of the problem. To combat these limitations, the algorithm is extended by a LP-based improvement procedure that is applied after generating a feasible truck schedule with the decoding procedure.

LP-based improvement procedure

The basic idea of the LP-based improvement procedure is to recalculate the number of unloaded parcels in each period after the starting and ending times of the inbound trucks have been fixed by the decoding procedure. This way, flexibility is reintroduced with regard to the number of unloaded parcels in each period as the number of unloaded parcels in each period is defined as a variable. Since the starting times z_i^{start} and ending times z_i^{end} of the inbound trucks remain fixed based on the schedule generated by the decoding procedure, the overall problem is reduced to a linear program. Here, the number of unloaded parcels in each period $x_{it}^{re} \geq 0$ constitute the only remaining (continuous) decision variables. To enforce the truck schedule, the parameter x_{it}^{up} is introduced which reflects the maximum number of unloaded parcels for each inbound as given by the truck schedule. Here, x_{it}^{up} is set to the maximum number of unloaded parcels set by the standard unloading speed x_i^{max} for those periods inbound i is unloaded in the given truck schedule and to 0 for the rest of the periods as given by the following formula.

$$
x_{it}^{up} = \begin{cases} x_i^{max}, & z_i^{start} \leq t \leq z_i^{end} \\ 0, & else \end{cases} \tag{5.2}
$$

Table 5.1 depicts the additional notation for the reduced formulation of the PHSP-LCC-flex.

Table 5.1.: Additional notation for the reduced PHSP-LCC-flex

Parameters	
x_{it}^{up}	maximum number of unloaded parcels for inbound i in period t

Decision variables	
$x_{it}^{re} \geq 0$	number of parcels unloaded from inbound truck i in period t

Since the given truck schedule already includes a feasible gate assignment of the inbound trucks, we do not have to consider the gate capacity in the reduced formulation. The truck schedule also guarantees a feasible unloading process for each individual inbound truck as the decoding procedure schedules the inbound trucks without allowing preemption. Thus, the reduced formulation only has to encompass restrictions concerning conveyor capacity, complete unloading of the inbound trucks and the maximum number of unloaded parcels each period. The model for the reduced formulation of the PHSP-LCC-flex is formally defined as follows.

Reduced Model for the PHSP-LCC-flex

$$max \ Z = \sum_{o \in \mathcal{O}} \sum_{t=1}^{dl_o - 1} \sum_{i \in \mathcal{I}_t} x_{it}^{re} \cdot \frac{ship_{io}}{l_i} \tag{5.3}$$

subject to

$$\sum_{i \in \mathcal{I}_t} x_{it}^{re} \cdot \frac{lk_{ik}}{l_i} \leq r_k \qquad \forall k \in \mathcal{K}, \forall t \in \mathcal{T} \setminus \{T\} \tag{5.4}$$

$$\sum_{t \in \mathcal{T}_i} x_{it}^{re} = l_i \qquad \forall i \in I \tag{5.5}$$

$$x_{it}^{re} \leq x_{it}^{up} \qquad \forall i \in \mathcal{I}, \forall t \in \mathcal{T}_i \setminus \{T\} \tag{5.6}$$

$$x_{it}^{re} \geq 0 \qquad \forall i \in \mathcal{I}, \forall t \in \mathcal{T}_i \tag{5.7}$$

The objective function (5.3) maximizes the number of non-delayed parcels. Constraints (5.4) restrict the number unloaded parcels for each conveyor k to the conveyor capacity. Constraints (5.5) ensure that each inbound truck is fully unloaded. The given truck schedule is enforced by restrictions (5.6). Lastly, equations (5.7) define x_{it}^{re} as a positive continuous variable. To show the effects of applying the improvement procedure, we again consider the exemplary instance with 19 inbound trucks, 27 outbounds, 8 inbound gates and 4 conveyors again. Applying the procedure results in the truck schedule and conveyor utilization shown in Figure 5.10.

Using the LP-based improvement procedure results in no changes with regard to the truck schedule as it does not influence the starting and ending times of the individual inbound trucks. The fixed starting and ending times of the inbound trucks also only allow for minor variations in the total number of unloaded parcels in each period and thus only lead to small changes in the conveyor utilization, especially a higher utilization of conveyor 3. These minor variations do, however, influence the number of non-delayed parcels and the number of parcels arriving before their respective deadlines rises from $\sum_o U_o = 8281$ to $\sum_o U_o = 8587$. Thus, the LP-based improvement procedure is capable of improving the objective function value by making use of the offered flexibility for the exemplary instance.

To conclude, two of the three main limitations of the decoding procedure are addressed by the LP-based improvement procedure as it does consider

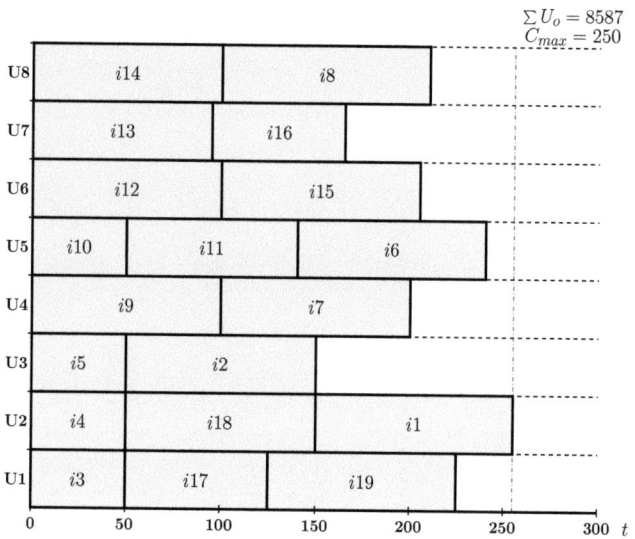

(a) Optimized schedule

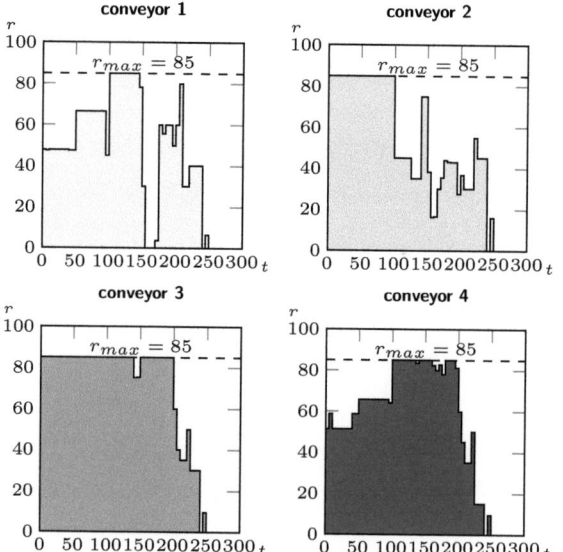

(b) Optimized conveyor utilization

Figure 5.10.: Truck schedule and conveyor utilization with LP-based improvement

the deadlines of outbound trucks and allows for a higher degree of flexibility regarding the number of unloaded parcels. However, the LP-based improvement procedure still does not allow for intended delays in the unloading process as the starting and ending times are exclusively determined by the decoding procedure. Thus, even when applying the LP-based improvement procedure only a subsection of the overall solution space of the problem is covered by the random-key representation of the solution. Consequentially, for some instances an optimal solution might not be covered by the representation. The representation can however still be used to find good solutions quickly. The performance of the algorithm is further investigated in Section 5.3 on page 103.

5.2.4. Initial population

The initial population for genetic algorithms often consists of randomly generated individuals. More sophisticated approaches exist that use sampling techniques to avoid an initial population only partially covering the solution space. The initial population can also be complemented with solutions that are known to be good.[18]

The genetic algorithm for the PHSP-LCC-flex also uses a randomly generated initial population and supplements it with a solution that reflects the FCFS-sequence of the inbound trucks. We can generate a random solution of the initial population in random-key representation by drawing a random real value from the interval $[0, 1)$ for each inbound truck. For the solution based on the FCFS-sequence each random key we first assign a rank $R(i)$ to each inbound truck according to their arrival time. If more than one inbound truck arrive at the same time, they are sorted according to the smallest index rule. The random key of each inbound truck is then calculated by normalizing the ranks in the interval $[0, 1)$. The method is shown in Algorithm 5.3.

---

[18]Glover and Kochenberger (2006).

Algorithm 5.3: Generating initial solution based on FCFS-sequence

---

Input: Instance
$$P = (\mathcal{I}, \mathcal{O}, \mathcal{K}, \mathcal{T}, U, r_k, x_i^{max}, l_i, lk_{ik}, dl_o, ship_{io}, at_i)$$
Output: Random-Key Solution λ

1 initialize empty vector of random keys λ
2 sort inbound trucks according to their arrival time at_i in sequence
   seq
3 $it = 1$
4 **for** $i \in seq$ **do**
5 $\quad\bigg|\quad \lambda_i = \frac{it}{\sum_{ii=1}^{I} ii} = \frac{2 \cdot it}{|\mathcal{I}| \cdot (|\mathcal{I}|+1)}$
6 $\quad\bigg|\quad$ $it = it + 1$

First ranking the inbound trucks and then normalizing them over the interval $[0, 1)$ has the advantage of creating a solution in random-key representation that encompasses values from the whole interval of possible random keys. This allows for more diverse solutions throughout the application of the genetic algorithm.

5.2.5. Evolutionary strategy

Selection and crossover

To generate new individuals for the subsequent generation, the first step is to select a pair of individuals from the current population. These two individuals are then subjected to the crossover operator with the result of generating new individuals or *offspring*. Selecting a specific crossover operator and selection method for the implementation of a genetic algorithm requires problem-specific considerations as both the crossover operator and selection method are dependent on the representation of the solution.[19]

For a solution in random-key representation, the combination of an *elitist*[20] selection strategy with the parameterized uniform crossover operator[21] constitutes a popular approach. This approach is also frequently designated as a *biased random-key genetic algorithm*[22] and favours in-

---

[19]Rothlauf (2011, p. 115).
[20]D. E. Goldberg (1989).
[21]Spears and De Jong (1995, p. 3).
[22]Gonçalves and Resende (2011, p. 487).

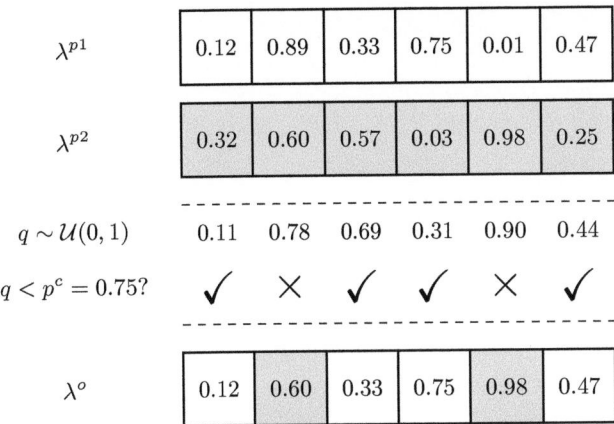

Figure 5.11.: Crossover for two exemplary solutions in random-key representation with $p^c = 0.75$

dividuals with higher fitness in the reproduction process for both the selection procedure and the crossover operator. The fittest individuals of the current population are designated as the *elite*. Each time two parents are selected for the crossover operator, one of those individuals has to be taken from the *elite*. Individuals can also be selected more than once for reproduction in each generation. The second individual is randomly selected from the rest of the current population. When two individuals are selected as parents, we apply the crossover operator to generate a single offspring. We generate a uniformly distributed random number from the interval $[0, 1]$ $q \sim \mathcal{U}(0, 1)$ for each random key λ_i of the solution and compare it with the selection probability. If the generated value is smaller than p^c, the respective random key λ_i^o of the offspring receives the random key of the first (elite) parent λ_i^{p1}. Otherwise, λ_i^o is set to the respective random key of the second parent λ_i^{p2}. Applying the crossover operator for two exemplary solutions with selection probability $p^c = 0.75$ is illustrated in Figure 5.11.

As observable in the example, the offspring only inherits the second and fourth key of the second parent whereas the remaining keys stem from the first *elite* parent. Generally, offspring created by the crossover operator usually resemble the first parent selected from the *elite* part of the population more. Thus, the decoded truck schedule and fitness is also closer to the *elite* parent solution and the algorithm tends to find

new solutions close to local optima. However, favouring solutions from
the *elite* part of the population also leads to a lower degree of diversity
in the population. To avoid remaining in local optima and to enhance
the diversity of the population, it is crucial to apply a suitable mutation
operator.[23]

Mutation

For a given population with solutions in random-key representation, we
only observe a limited number of distinct values for the random keys. In
case the genetic algorithm does not introduce new random-key values
throughout its execution, the total reachable solution space of the initial
population will be sampled after a sufficiently large number of iterations.[24]
Thus, to avoid premature convergence, new random-key values should be
introduced to the population with the mutation operator.

The mutation operator can either target specific genes, in this case
specific random-key values, or create entirely new solutions. As we
employ an *elitist* selecting scheme and a biased crossover operator, the
mutation operator for the genetic algorithm for the PHSP-LCC-flex has
to counteract the strong tendency to generate a prematurely converging
population. To enhance population diversity as much as possible, we
introduce new randomly generated solutions in each generation. Here,
the same generation procedure is used as for the initial population.
Since newly generated individuals mostly consist of novel random-key
values and are then paired with individuals form the *elite* part of the
population through the crossover operator we can avoid remaining in
local optima.

5.2.6. Selection procedure

Figure 5.12 shows the selection procedure between generations. The
population is sorted according to the individual fitness values at the end
of the generation and the fittest solutions are assigned to the *elite* part
of the population. Those *elite* individuals are directly copied into the
following generation. Since the fittest solutions are always transferred
to the next generation, the best found solution generally monotonically
improves. The largest part of the population in a new generation consists

---

[23]Mendes et al. (2009, p. 97).
[24]Mendes et al. (2009, p. 98).

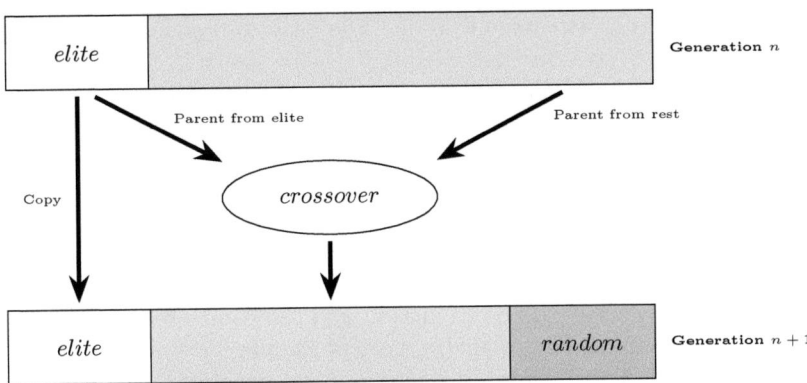

Figure 5.12.: Selection between generations

of offspring created through the crossover operator that inherit most of their genes from *elite* individuals. These individuals are usually quite similar to the *elite* individuals with regard to their fitness and the structure of their truck schedules. The remainder consists of newly generated individuals (mutants). Before the generation and selection of new individuals, the population is sorted according to their fitness again so newly generated individuals can enter the *elite* part of the next generation if their fitness is higher than the fitness of their parents.

Generally, the procedure leads to a fast convergence to local optima through the preferential treatment of good solution and still allows for a high degree of population diversity due to the rigorous mutation operator.

5.3. Numeric analysis of the genetic algorithm

5.3.1. Test design

The test instances originally presented in Section 4.5.1 on page 65 are considered again to assess the performance of the genetic algorithm illustrated in this chapter. Accordingly, the test set still includes a total of 810 test instances with varying levels of conveyor capacity and gate scarcity as well as different levels of heterogeinity of parcel destinations and dispersion of deadlines.

We consider three variants of the algorithm. All variants are implemented using programming language Python. The basic variant of the genetic algorithm GA^{base} uses the basic decoding scheme shown in Algorithm 5.2 without the LP-based improvement procedure of Section 19. The second variant GA^{base+} only employs the LP-based improvement procedure for the remaining individuals of the last iteration whereas the solution of the individuals of all other generations is decoded and evaluated by the basic decoding scheme. Finally, the third variant GA^{LP} utilizes the LP-based improvement procedure for every individual in every generation. For all variants of the genetic algorithm the population size is set to N = 50 individuals. For the reproduction and selection process, 20% of individuals are taken from the *elite* part of the population and 70% of the individuals of the following generation are generated through the crossover operator. The remaining 10% of the population consists of randomly generated mutants. The selection probability is $p^s = 0.7$ for all instances.

The performance of the variants of the genetic algorithm is evaluated with reference to the best known solution to the individual instances calculated by the standard solver Gurobi in the numeric study illustrated in Section 4.5 using a time limit of 3600 seconds. The termination criterion is a time limit of 30 seconds for all variants of the genetic algorithm. Further, the best found solution by Gurobi after the same time limit of 30 seconds is presented as a reference as well. The linear programs of the LP-based improvement procedure are also solved with Gurobi. All computations are conducted on a computer with a 3.60 GHz Intel Core i7-4790 processor and 16 gigabytes of RAM.

5.3.2. Numeric results

Table 5.2 shows the results for the basic variant of the genetic algorithm GA^{base} and the second variant GA^{base+} that includes applying the LP-improvement procedure in the last generation. The entries show the average relative gap to the best known solution generated by Gurobi for the given combination of the parameters σ and β. Each line thus represents 45 instances. Each column shows the results for a given time limit $\bar{t}= 1, ..., 30$ seconds. Further, the average gap after the application of the LP-based improvement procedure (GA^{base+}) and for solving the instances using Gurobi and a time limit of 30 seconds (Gurobi) are presented. For the small instances, we can observe that the basic genetic algorithm GA^{base} without the LP-based improvement procedure does

Table 5.2.: Deviation from the best known solution in [%] for the variants GA^{base} and GA^{base+}

			Genetic Algorithm GA^{base}							GA^{base+}	Gurobi
size	σ	β	$\bar{t}=1$	$\bar{t}=5$	$\bar{t}=10$	$\bar{t}=15$	$\bar{t}=20$	$\bar{t}=25$	$\bar{t}=30$	$\bar{t}=30$	$\bar{t}=30$
	0.9	0.9	4.59	2.37	2.04	1.93	1.84	1.80	1.76	1.42	2.70
	1.0	0.9	2.20	0.98	0.84	0.73	0.69	0.67	0.62	0.56	1.94
	1.1	0.9	0.62	0.15	0.11	0.11	0.09	0.08	0.07	0.07	0.42
	0.9	1.0	5.40	3.11	2.73	2.56	2.45	2.42	2.41	1.80	1.97
small	1.0	1.0	3.59	2.09	1.89	1.79	1.71	1.68	1.65	1.45	2.13
	1.1	1.0	2.09	1.35	1.26	1.21	1.19	1.17	1.15	0.91	1.36
	0.9	1.1	5.57	3.32	2.93	2.73	2.66	2.60	2.58	1.82	1.05
	1.0	1.1	3.38	2.03	1.81	1.72	1.69	1.67	1.64	1.31	0.88
	1.1	1.1	2.38	1.62	1.47	1.42	1.40	1.38	1.36	0.94	0.50
$\varnothing$			3.31	1.89	1.68	1.58	1.52	1.50	1.47	1.14	1.44
	0.9	0.9	4.97	3.29	2.48	2.12	1.90	1.80	1.73	1.40	4.95
	1.0	0.9	1.61	0.81	0.47	0.35	0.30	0.28	0.25	0.25	1.80
	1.1	0.9	1.02	0.29	0.13	0.08	0.06	0.05	0.04	0.04	1.00
	0.9	1.0	5.33	3.74	3.04	2.57	2.35	2.25	2.17	1.78	2.94
large	1.0	1.0	2.74	1.86	1.30	1.12	1.02	0.96	0.94	0.85	3.49
	1.1	1.0	0.87	0.34	0.18	0.13	0.11	0.11	0.09	0.09	1.44
	0.9	1.1	5.60	4.36	3.54	3.1	2.82	2.69	2.61	1.98	1.95
	1.0	1.1	4.00	3.03	2.54	2.29	2.16	2.10	2.05	1.57	2.53
	1.1	1.1	3.35	2.68	2.39	2.24	2.16	2.10	2.06	1.65	2.53
$\varnothing$			3.28	2.27	1.79	1.56	1.43	1.37	1.32	1.08	2.51

on average perform slightly worse using a time limit of 30 seconds with an average gap of 1.47 % compared to Gurobi with 1.44 %. Especially for instances with $\beta = 1.1$ and thus having a lower level of gate scarcity, Gurobi finds better solutions on average if a time limit of 30 seconds is used. However, using the LP-based improvement procedure for the last generation of the genetic algorithm does result in a lower average gap of 1.14 % for the smaller instances and 1.08 % for the larger instances. In comparison, solving with Gurobi using a time limit of 30 seconds results in an average gap of 1.44 % for the smaller instances and 1.08 % for the larger instances. For the instances with $\beta = 1.1$, the average gap is also much closer to the reference value of Gurobi with a time limit of 30 seconds. For the larger instances, the basic genetic algorithm performs better than Gurobi on average for nearly all instances. Moreover, the LP-based improvement procedure is also able to lower the gap further. With regard to the progression of the gap over the execution time of the algorithm, the largest improvements are generally seen at the beginning between 1 and 5 seconds and diminish afterwards.

Table 5.3 illustrates the average relative gap from the best known solution for the third variant of the genetic algorithm GA^{LP} that employs the

Table 5.3.: Deviation from the best known solution in [%] for variant GA^{LP}

| size | σ | β | Genetic Algorithm GA^{LP} | | | | | | | Gurobi |
			$\bar{t}=1$	$\bar{t}=5$	$\bar{t}=10$	$\bar{t}=15$	$\bar{t}=20$	$\bar{t}=25$	$\bar{t}=30$	$\bar{t}=30$
	0.9	0.9	5.13	3.43	2.44	1.98	1.81	1.68	1.60	2.70
	1.0	0.9	3.33	1.95	1.34	1.09	0.99	0.91	0.84	1.94
	1.1	0.9	1.24	0.56	0.27	0.19	0.17	0.15	0.13	0.42
	0.9	1.0	4.52	3.15	2.35	1.97	1.70	1.58	1.46	1.97
small	1.0	1.0	3.61	2.40	1.77	1.52	1.38	1.27	1.23	2.13
	1.1	1.0	2.34	1.62	1.19	1.05	0.96	0.89	0.86	1.36
	0.9	1.1	4.20	2.66	1.96	1.60	1.41	1.27	1.18	1.05
	1.0	1.1	2.84	1.87	1.26	1.07	0.94	0.83	0.79	0.88
	1.1	1.1	1.91	1.26	0.86	0.68	0.63	0.58	0.55	0.50
$\varnothing$			**3.24**	**2.10**	**1.49**	**1.24**	**1.11**	**1.02**	**0.96**	**1.44**
	0.9	0.9	4.92	4.18	3.59	3.11	2.77	2.54	2.30	4.95
	1.0	0.9	2.00	1.41	1.06	0.77	0.63	0.53	0.46	1.80
	1.1	0.9	1.33	0.86	0.51	0.32	0.20	0.15	0.12	1.00
	0.9	1.0	4.52	3.71	3.20	2.95	2.73	2.54	2.40	2.94
large	1.0	1.0	2.74	2.23	1.83	1.65	1.45	1.33	1.21	3.49
	1.1	1.0	1.11	0.76	0.52	0.37	0.31	0.24	0.19	1.44
	0.9	1.1	4.06	3.37	2.98	2.76	2.53	2.33	2.09	1.95
	1.0	1.1	3.12	2.61	2.31	2.11	1.97	1.85	1.74	2.53
	1.1	1.1	2.72	2.42	2.16	2.02	1.90	1.80	1.69	2.53
$\varnothing$			**2.72**	**2.42**	**2.16**	**2.02**	**1.90**	**1.80**	**1.69**	**2.51**

LP-based improvement procedure for each individual in every generation. Each row again shows the results for the instances with the given combination of β and σ. For both the smaller and larger instances, the genetic algorithm GA^{LP} performs better on average with an average gap 1.14 % for the small instances and 1.08 % for the large instances compared to Gurobi with a time limit of 30 seconds.

Comparing the results of the first and second variant GA^{base} and GA^{base+} of the genetic algorithm with the third variant GA^{LP}, we can observe that the third variant GA^{LP} performs better on average for the smaller instances and worse on average for the larger instances. This can be attributed to the number of generations that can be evaluated throughout the execution of the algorithm. The variant GA^{LP} takes longer than the basic variant GA^{base} to evaluate each individual since a linear program has to be solved every time. Here, solving the respective linear program takes comparatively longer for the larger instances. Accordingly, the GA^{LP} generally finds better solutions within the first seconds but cannot decrease the gap as significantly as the basic variant GA^{base} for the larger instances.

For further insights on the performance of the three variants of the genetic algorithm in specific circumstances, refer to Figure 5.13. The figure shows the results for fixed values of the instance parameters α, μ, σ and β, respectively. Each bar illustrates the average relative gap to the best known solution using the three variants of the genetic algorithm and Gurobi with a time limit of 30 second for the instances of both the smaller and larger category with the given parameter value for α, μ, σ and β respectively, thus 135 instances each.

We can observe that with regard to the parcel destination heterogeneity α, instances with a higher value for α and thus parcels designated for a larger number of destinations seem to be slightly easier to solve for both instance sizes and all three variants of the genetic algorithm. Concerning the deadline distribution μ, we can only observe a negligible impact on the performance of the genetic algorithm of different values for the parameter. However, the performance of Gurobi is affected by the deadline distribution as it has less difficulty solving instances with less spread out deadlines ($\mu = 0.1$). Instances with scarce conveyor capacities seem to be harder to solve overall than those with less constrained capacities as we see a monotonically decreasing average gap form instances with $\sigma = 0.9$ to those with $\sigma = 1.1$ for both instance sizes. The gate scarcity appears to have the reverse effect on the performance of the genetic algorithm and Gurobi, instances with higher values of β and thus more gates are mostly solved with a smaller average gap.

To summarize, all variants of the genetic algorithm can find better solutions for most instances compared to Gurobi with a time limit of 30 seconds. The variants GA^{base+} and GA^{LP} dominate the variant GA^{base} however. For larger instances the study indicates that it is beneficial to employ the variant GA^{base+} and thus to only use the LP-based improvement procedure for the last generation. For smaller instances using the variant GA^{LP} and utilizing the LP-based improvement procedure for each individual outperforms the GA^{base+} variant.

From a practical point of view, all variants of the algorithm generate solutions with high quality. Accordingly, the differences between the variants is relatively minor.

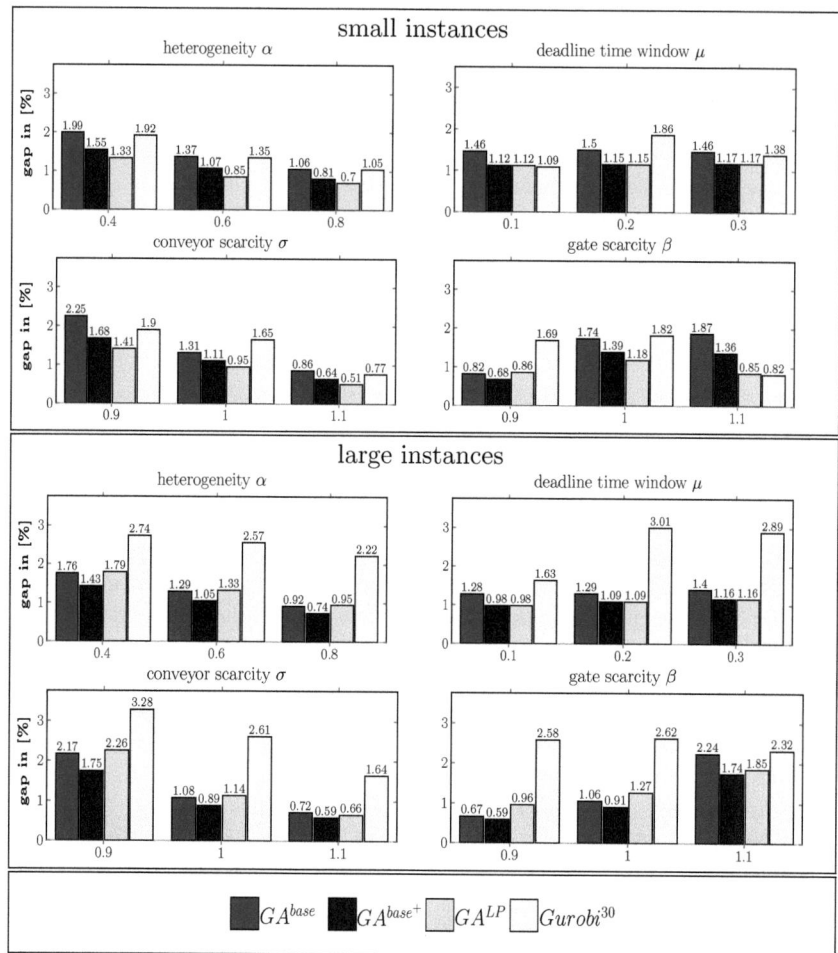

Figure 5.13.: Comparison of the configurations of the genetic algorithm with a time limit of 30 seconds

6. Evaluation of truck schedules at parcel hubs with a simulation model

6.1. Purpose of the simulation model

6.1.1. Motivation for using simulation as an evaluation tool

The mathematical models illustrated in Chapter 4 assume a deterministic view on the truck scheduling problem at parcel hubs. However, in a practical setting the problem exhibits several components that are subjected to stochastic variations such as uncertainties concerning the arrival of trucks or the availability of resources at the hub. Generally, uncertainties are often intentionally neglected when approaching the truck scheduling problem with a deterministic view - mainly since dealing with stochastic variations comes with significant additional challenges.[1]

This leads to the questions if and how the results of deterministic optimization models of the problem are applicable to a stochastic setting. To answer this question, a discrete-event simulation framework is employed to evaluate the quality of solutions determined with the deterministic methods illustrated in the previous chapters.

6.1.2. Incorporated stochastic system components

In a real-world environment, the internal and external components of the truck scheduling problem at cross docks is often subjected to operational uncertainties. Figure 6.1 illustrates potential sources of internal and external uncertainty.

---

[1] Ardakani and Fei (2020, p. 3).

Table 6.1.: Internal and external uncertainties in cross docking based on
Ardakani and Fei (2020)

Operational Uncertainties	
internal	external
processing time	demand
departure time	supply
available resources	arrival time
	truck availability

For an overview of problem settings and approaches to deal with uncertainties in cross docking refer to Ardakani and Fei (2020) or Walha
et al. (2014). The focus of their work lies on investigating stochastic
transfer and unloading processes. In prior studies on uncertain processing
times, Wang and Regan (2008) and McWilliams (2009a) investigate how
methods that consider uncertain arrival times influence the transshipment
times inside the hub. Further, Sathasivan (2011) assume variations in
the unloading times due to different skill sets of workers, the number of
concurrently unloaded trucks and other factors.

In the following, another source of uncertainty in the unloading process is
examined - namely, the uncertain loading patterns and uncertain parcel
composition of trucks and their impact on conveyor utilization in the
special case of parcel hubs. More precisely, the parcel flow originating
from an inbound truck during the unloading process is mostly heterogeneous since the parcels are arbitrary loaded. Thus, parcels leave the
trucks in a random sequence. Especially in situations when specific parcel
flows interact with the flows from concurrently unloaded inbound trucks
we may observe an accumulation of transfers for a specific conveyor.
Thus, the workload on the conveyors is subjected to stochastic variations
induced by the unloading sequences of the parcels. Further, the parcel
composition concerning the destinations is only partially known which
increases the variability of the realized parcel flows.

In the mathematical models of Chapter 4, individual parcels and detailed
interactions between the parcels are not considered and a homogenized
parcel flow is assumed. With respect to the mathematical model, the
detailed inclusion of parcel interactions would render it intractable with
regard to the required computational effort for solving the model. Further, the lack of information on the exact composition of each inbound

truck is another argument against including them in the deterministic mathematical formulation. However, including parcel interactions in a simulation model is possible. In the following, a discrete-event simulation model is developed to investigate how well the optimized truck schedules generated by the mathematical models perform under the assumption of heterogeneous unloading sequences. A brief overview of the combined application of simulation and optimization in the context of operating and designing cross docks is given first.

6.1.3. Combining optimization and simulation

Simulation and optimization can be combined in several different ways. Several approaches to categorize the combination of simulation and optimization are discussed in the literature. According to Fu (2002) two basic concepts can be employed when using simulation and optimization together: (*1*) simulation for optimization or (*2*) optimization for simulation. For case (*1*) an optimization subroutine generates candidate solutions for a simulation model whereas for case (*2*) a simulation generates scenarios as input for an optimization model.[2] Ladier et al. (2014b) elaborate on the concept in the context of cross dock scheduling problems and specify four ways simulation and optimization models can interact.[3] They distinguish between applications where optimization and simulation are embedded with each other or generate input for another as shown in Figure 6.1.

---

[2]Fu (2002, p. 194).
[3]Ladier et al. (2014b, p. 2).

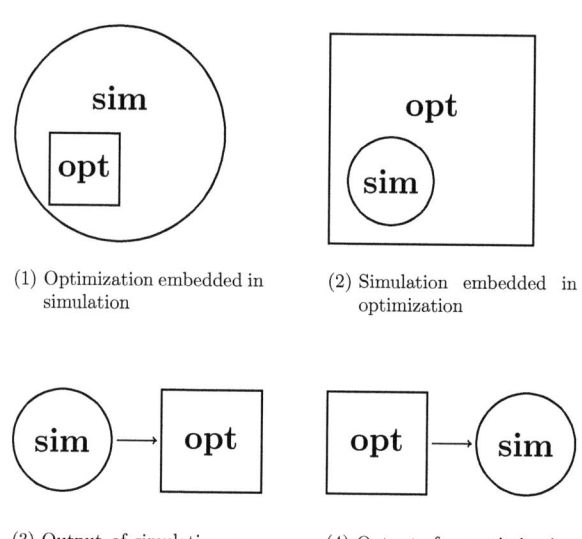

(1) Optimization embedded in simulation

(2) Simulation embedded in optimization

(3) Output of simulation model as input in optimization model

(4) Output of an optimization model as input in simulation model

Figure 6.1.: Combined use of optimization and simulation models based on Ladier et al., 2014b

(1) **Optimization embedded in simulation**

When embedding optimization in simulation, a superordinated simulation model uses an optimization model as a subroutine for decision support during the simulation process. The relationship is often recursive and thus the subroutine is executed more than once in many applications. In the context of cross docking, Clausen et al. (2012) simulate the operations in a less-than-truckload network and use a mathematical model to optimize the routing of shipments to the individual hubs of the network. Another example are Cox and Rossetti (2017) who simulate the operations at a manual post distribution center and use an optimization model to generate staff schedules. Wang and Regan (2008) also use the concept of embedding optimization in simulation to schedule incoming trucks in real-time as part of an *Arena* simulation model. Gue (1999) use a linear program to determine the freight flows inside a cross dock as part of a simulation model that evaluates the effectiveness of particular hub layouts.

(2) **Simulation embedded in optimization**

For many real-world problem settings, computing performance measures and finding optimal solutions analytically is very challenging. Here, a potential approach is to employ simulation as an evaluation tool and to use the results for optimization. The relationship between the simulation and optimization model here is also mostly recursive. The concept is frequently referred to as *simulation optimization* and used for a variety of applications.[4] Refer to Amaran et al. (2016) or Tekin and Sabuncuoglu (2004) for an overview of applications and methods of simulation optimization.

Regarding cross docking, McWilliams (2005) minimize the makespan of transfer operations at a parcel hub with a mixed integer program and evaluate the solutions by simulating the transfer operations. Similarly, Clausen et al. (2015) also use a mixed integer program to optimize the assignment of inbound trucks at a cross docking hub to balance the workload on the internal conveyors. They use a simulation model to calculate the resulting workload of a given truck schedule. Aickelin and Adewunmi (2006) apply the concept to the dock-door-assignment problem and solve it with a local search algorithm where a simulation model evaluates the objective function during each iteration. Another example for the integration of a simulation model as an evaluation tool for a heuristic solution method

---

[4] Andradóttir (1998, p. 151).

is Wu et al. (2011) who minimize the combined transportation, inventory holding and back order penalty costs for the operations of a cross dock.

(3) **Output of simulation model as input in optimization model**
In some cases, simulation models can generate the required data for optimization models. Hauser (2002) uses a simulation model to generate different suitable hub layouts that are integrated in a genetic algorithm for a dock-door-assignment problem where the walking distances for the internal operations are minimized and workload is balanced. With regard to personnel planning at cross docking hubs, Liu and Takakuwa (2009) generate data on the required daily workload that is used as input for a mixed integer program to generate optimized personnel schedules.

(4) **Output of optimization model as input in simulation model**
For this concept, the simulation model is mainly used as an evaluation tool for the solutions of an optimization model, frequently to test the feasibility or robustness of, e.g., an optimized schedule with regard to uncertainties or factors that are not included in the optimization model. Thus, it is mostly applied in a stochastic setting or to test the influence of modelling simplifications.[5] Refer to Ladier et al. (2014b) for an overview of challenges when using simulation as an evaluation tool for optimization problems. To investigate uncertainties in cross docking applications, Ladier et al. (2014a) use a simulation model to test the robustness of inbound truck schedules assuming uncertain arrival times of the inbound trucks. Further simulation-based evaluations of schedule robustness are found in Ladier and Alpan (2016b) for a problem setting with time windows and in Zouhaier and Said (2017) who use methods from the field of queuing theory to model inbound truck handling at the hub. With regard to investigating the effect of model simplifications, Gambardella et al. (1998) propose a mixed integer program to optimize the resource allocation inside of an inter-modal container hub and use a simulation model to evaluate the feasibility of the solution.

For the remainder of this work a solution framework for solving the PHSP following a concept akin to using the output of optimization model as input in simulation model (4) is presented. In this regard, the different mathematical models with varying assumptions from Chapter 4 are solved

---

[5]Bachelet and Yon (2007, p. 704).

for a set of test instances and the solutions are then evaluated using a simulation model. The simulation model is introduced in the following section and follows the descriptions found in Bugow and Kellenbrink (2023).

6.2. Discrete-event simulation model of the parcel hub

6.2.1. General structure of the simulation model

To simulate variety of different parcel hubs in several operational settings, a flexible simulation framework is required. Thus, instead of using a commercial simulation software, the simulation model is implemented using a custom-made framework programmed in Python that can be adjusted for different settings easily. Further, the custom simulation model allows for the application of optimized truck schedules and the detailed implementation of uncertain unloading sequences. Formally, the simulation model is designed according to the discrete-event paradigm and includes system variables or entities that change their state only at discrete points in time when events occur.[6] For parcel hubs, the main entities are the inbound trucks and parcels. The system entities possess attributes that characterize them and determine how they respond in specific circumstances. An exemplary attribute would be the destination of a parcel. Entities also frequently require resources to change their state such as a free gate for arriving inbound trucks. Events reference occurrences that lead to state changes of the entities and are processed according to an event list that specifies the sequence and time of the currently active events. An exemplary event would be the arrival of an inbound truck. The event list is updated after an event occurred and new events are potentially added. Events are processed until the event list is empty and the simulation ends.[7]

---

[6]Banks (2003, p. 663).
[7]Karnon et al. (2012, p. 702).

Table 6.2.: States and attributes of the model entities

Entity	‖ Attributes	States
inbound trucks	arrival time *starting time* number of loaded parcels *parcel sequence*	current position unloading status
outbound trucks	deadline	current loading status
gates		currently assigned truck
conveyors	capacity	current capacity usage
parcels	destination unloading speed	current position

6.2.2. Model entities, system states and events of the simulation model

To implement the discrete-event simulation model for the parcel hub scheduling problem, we first have to define the specific entities, their attributes and states and the events influencing the system state. The relevant model entities and their attributes and states are shown in Table 6.2.

Attributes of the entities are defined exogenously and remain unchanged during the simulation run. Some attributes are however not part of the instance data and change from one simulation run to another, namely the starting time of the inbound trucks and the parcel sequence. The starting time refers to the point in time an inbound truck starts unloading its cargo and is dependent on the scheduling policy for the inbound trucks. The set of possible scheduling policies ranges from basic policies such as the FCFS rule to more advanced forms such as those based on the solutions of mathematical models, i.e, the solutions to the problems modeled in the previous chapters. Scheduling policies are illustrated in more detail in Section 6.2.3. The sequence in which parcels leave the individual inbound truck is uncertain as described in Section 6.1.2. For the purposes of the simulation, a random sequence is determined for the parcels once an inbound truck has been assigned to a gate.

To model the dynamics of the system four distinct events $e \in E$ are introduced:

(I) Arriving inbound truck

(II) Departing inbound truck

(III) Unload parcel from inbound truck

(IV) Load parcel to outbound truck

They appear on the event list $EL(t^c)$ at the current simulation time t^c with a corresponding event time t^e and change current system state $ST(t^c)$ to the new system state $ST(t^n)$. The system state encompasses the states of all entities shown in Table 6.2. An overview of the four relevant events is given in Figure 6.2.

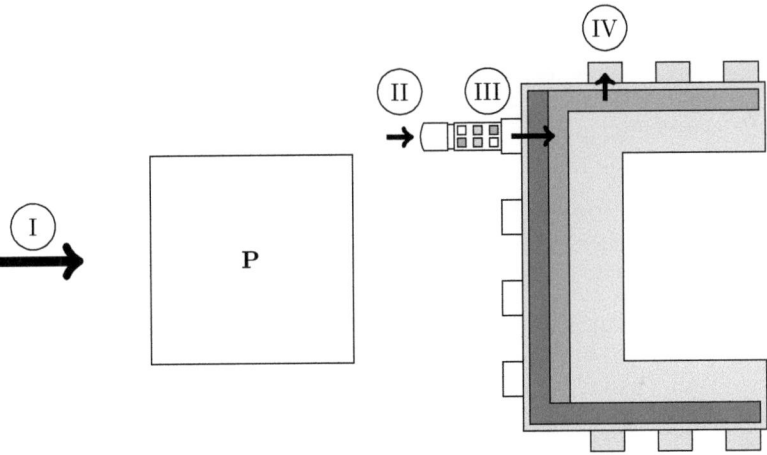

Figure 6.2.: Events in the simulation model

A detailed description of the interaction of events and states is illustrated in Appendix A.

6.2.3. Scheduling policies

The potential states and dynamics of the system are generally defined by the entities and events of the simulation model. However, at some points during the simulation run, e.g., when an inbound truck leaves a gate, decisions have to be taken on the scheduling of the trucks - namely when to start unloading the individual inbound trucks. These decisions can be implemented using scheduling policies that define which truck is selected for unloading at the relevant points in time. These policies can include priority-based rules that sequence trucks according to a priority measurement such as their arrival time or more complex rules based on the results of mathematical models such as those presented in Chapter 4. For the PHSP-LCC, we employ the results of the deterministic models illustrated in Chapter 4 to test their applicability in a stochastic setting. Naturally, the resulting truck schedules of the deterministic mathematical models are often not directly realizable in a stochastic environment. As uncertainties can induce delays throughout the execution of the plan, measures to react to deviations from the plan have to be devised. Thus, the starting times from the optimal solution of the models and the optimized unloading speeds for the PHSP-LCC-flex constitute the basis for several scheduling policies that are presented below. The following four scheduling policies are applied for the simulation of the PHSP-LCC.

(I) **First-Come-First-Served (FCFS):**
   Sort the inbound trucks in non-descending order according to their arrival time and assign them to a dock once it is free.

(II) **Starting Times of the PHSP-LCC-fix Model (Fix):**
   Use the starting times of the solution of the PHSP-LCC-fix model and assign the inbound trucks once a dock is free after their starting time.

(III) **Starting Times of the PHSP-LCC-flex model (Flex):**
   Use the starting times of the solution of the PHSP-LCC-flex model and assign the inbound trucks once a dock is free after their starting time.

(IV) **Starting Times and Unloading Speeds of the PHSP-LCC-flex model (Flex$^+$):**
   Use the starting times and the calculated unloading speeds of the solution of the PHSP-LCC-flex model and assign the inbound trucks once a dock is free after their starting time.

(V) **Starting Times and Priorities of the PHSP-LCC-flex model (Flex^{prio}):**
   Use the starting times of the solution of the PHSP-LCC-flex model and assign the inbound trucks once a dock is free after their starting time. In case a conveyor reaches its maximum capacities,

priorities those trucks that would have had to unload the highest number of parcels until the current time period according to the solution of the PHSP-LCC-flex model.

The FCFS rule is widely used in practice for cross dock scheduling due to its comparatively simple nature and easy applicability.[8] However, the FCFS rule does neither take the objective of minimizing the number of tardy parcels into account nor does it permit intended waiting times to allow more urgent trucks to be scheduled before trucks that are already present. The FCFS rule is used as a reference for the other policies for the remainder of this work. The *Fix* and *Flex* scheduling policies sort the inbound trucks according to their starting times in the solution of the respective mathematical model and schedule them according to the resulting sequence. Further, they only allow the inbound trucks to be unloaded if their optimized starting time has already passed. With regard to the unloading speed, both *Fix* and *Flex* do however assume that the parcels are unloaded with the fixed standard speed and do not allow for slower unloading speeds. For the $Flex^+$ policy the assumption is made that the unloading speeds are indeed controllable and both the starting times and unloading speeds of the PHSP-LCC-flex model are respected. Thus, each parcel receives an individual unloading speed that is calculated by dividing the number of unloaded parcels in a period by the period length. The inbound trucks are unloaded once their starting time has passed, as for the *Flex* policy.

Lastly, the $Flex^{prio}$ policy operates similarly to the *Flex* as it also schedules the inbound trucks according to the starting times taken form the solution of the PHSP-LCC-flex model. In contrast to the $Flex^+$ policy, it does not directly utilize the individual unloading speeds taken from the solution of the PHSP-LCC-flex model and all parcels are always unloaded with the standard unloading speed. However, it adds a priority rule based on the unloading speeds of the PHSP-LCC-flex model in case of a resource conflict occurs due to a conveyor reaching its maximum capacity. In this case, all parcels waiting to be unloaded to the conveyor that has reached its maximum capacity are put into a queue. Once the conveyor is not operating at its maximum capacity anymore, the parcels are sorted according to a priority value that is based on the solution of the PHSP-LCC-flex model. The priority value for a parcel originating

---

[8]Maknoon et al. (2014).

from inbound truck i in the time period corresponding to the current simulation time t' is calculated according to the following formula:

$$prio_{it'} = \sum_{t<t'} x_{it}^{opt} \qquad (6.1)$$

This way, trucks that would have had to unload the highest amount of parcels up until the current time period t' according to the solution of the PHSP-LCC-flex are unloaded first once a resource conflict occurs.

6.3. Exemplary application of the simulation model

6.3.1. Comparison of heterogeneous and homogeneous parcel flows

As already established, in a real-world setting the parcels in the inbound trucks are loaded according to arbitrary patterns and the resulting sequence of parcels during the unloading process is thus assumed to be random. This leads to a heterogeneous flow of parcels leaving the inbound trucks with regard to the destinations of the unloaded parcels. The parcel flows entering the conveyors inside the hub can then lead to accumulations of parcels for specific destinations and result in overloaded and blocked conveyors. In the mathematical models of Chapters 4 the parcel flows were assumed to be homogeneous as individual parcel interactions were not considered. It was assumed that the parcels would leave the inbound trucks evenly distributed during the unloading process. Naturally, these homogeneous parcel flows do not exhibit stochastic variations. The discrete-event simulation model of the parcel hub now does include the individual parcel interactions since the individual parcels are the main entities of the model. As a result, we can use the simulation model to investigate the influence of heterogeneous unloading sequences. The homogenization scheme is presented in Appendix B.

Figure 6.3 illustrates the resulting conveyor utilization when using the discrete-event simulation model with a FCFS scheduling policy while applying the homogenised unloading sequence for the exemplary instance already used in Chapter 4. Further, the conveyor utilization for two random unloading sequences are shown as a reference.

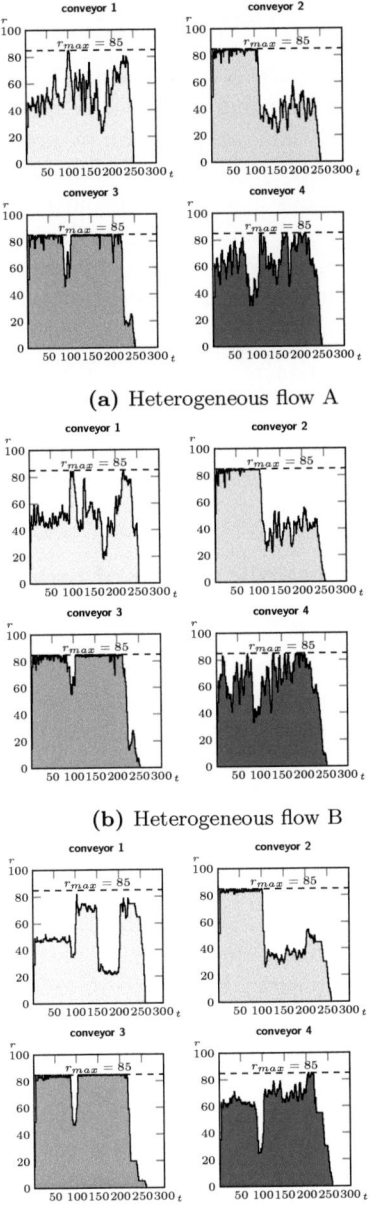

(a) Heterogeneous flow A

(b) Heterogeneous flow B

(c) Homogenised flow

Figure 6.3.: Conveyor utilization for homogenised and heterogeneous parcel flow

The corresponding makespan C_{max} when homogenizing the parcel flow with the conveyor utilization shown in Figure 6.3c equals 254 minutes and the number of non-delayed parcels $\sum_o U_o$ equals 7735 parcels. Figures 6.3a and 6.3b show the conveyor utilization for two exemplary trailer packing patterns A and B that result in two heterogeneous parcel unloading sequences when also applying FCFS scheduling policy. In all three cases the number and destinations of the parcels inside the inbound trucks are identical, only the sequence in which the parcels leave the truck differs. Especially on conveyor 1, we observe a visible difference with regard to the conveyor utilization. However, the resulting makespan $C_{max}^A = 245$ and $C_{max}^B = 248$ as well as the number of non-delayed parcels $\sum_o U_o^A = 7764$ and $\sum_o U_o^B = 7750$ for both unloading sequences are in the same range. Thus, using the simulation model with a a more homogenized unloading process does not always lead to significantly different makespan or number of tardy parcels.

6.3.2. Assessing the applicability of optimized truck schedules using scheduling policies

The exemplary and preliminary investigation of homogenized and heterogeneous unloading sequences shows a rather small influence of the unloading sequence on the objective when applying the FCFS scheduling policy. Smaller deviations in the unloading process can however have a greater influence on the applicability of the truck schedules generated by the mathematical models. The optimized truck schedules provide starting times for the unloading process of the individual inbound trucks in the case of the PHSP-LCC-fix. For the PHSP-LCC-flex, we also determine the number of unloaded parcels in each period. For heterogeneous unloading sequences, random accumulation of parcels for specific conveyors can be observed frequently. Due to these random accumulations, individual conveyors reach their capacity and parcels that are still in the inbound truck have to wait until the conveyor is free again. Thus, small delays manifest themselves and the starting times calculated using the mathematical models oftentimes cannot be realized in the simulation model. Then, we have to postpone the start of the unloading process for the respective inbound trucks. For this reason, the starting times of the inbound trucks calculated with the mathematical models are used as earliest starting times for the simulation model for the *Fix*, *Flex*,

$Flex^+$ and $Flex^{prio}$ scheduling policy. Postponing the unloading process of one inbound truck has an influence on the following trucks leading to a propagation of delays throughout the planning horizon.

To demonstrate the resulting deviations from the optimized truck schedules calculated with the mathematical models we utilize the exemplary instance from Chapter 4 on page 31. Figure 6.6 shows the schedules and resulting conveyor utilization when applying the PHSP-LCC-fix and the Fix scheduling policy with homogenized and heterogeneous unloading sequences.

Comparing the schedules generated for the exemplary instance using the PHSP-LCC-fix model with those of the simulation with the Fix policy shows that we obtain similar results when assuming homogenized unloading sequences. The resulting makespan is identical with $C_{max} = 250$ and the number of parcels on time only deviates slightly with $\sum_o U_o^{opt} = 9600$ and $\sum_o U_o^{hom} = 9590$. The slight differences can be attributed to the discretization of the parcel flow in the simulation as we consider single parcels instead of a combined parcel flow as in the mathematical models. We can observe the effects of discretization when closer examining the conveyor utilization for the model results in Figure 6.4b and the simulation with homogeneous unloading sequences in Figure 6.8b. Here, the utilization follows a step function for the model results whereas the utilization in the simulation constitutes a smoothed version of the step function of the model results. At first glance, the schedules in Figure 6.4a and Figure 6.5a seem to differ considerably. The differences can however be attributed to smaller deviations in the duration of the individual unloading processes of the inbound trucks that force succeeding inbound trucks to be scheduled at another gate. These gates are only available since the optimized schedule left free gate capacities throughout the planning horizon in the optimal solution of the mathematical model.

The simulation results for heterogeneous unloading patterns are shown in Figure 6.6a and Figure 6.9b. We can observe stark differences with regard to the makespan of $C_{max}^{het} = 254$ and number of parcels without delay $\sum_o U_o^{het} = 8993$ compared to the results assuming homogeneous unloading patterns. The randomized unloading sequences frequently lead to overloaded conveyors and thus a halt in the unloading process of the corresponding inbound trucks. Consequently, the unloading process of succeeding inbound trucks have to be postponed and an increased number of parcels arrives at the outbounds after the deadline. The results are however still significantly better with regard to the number

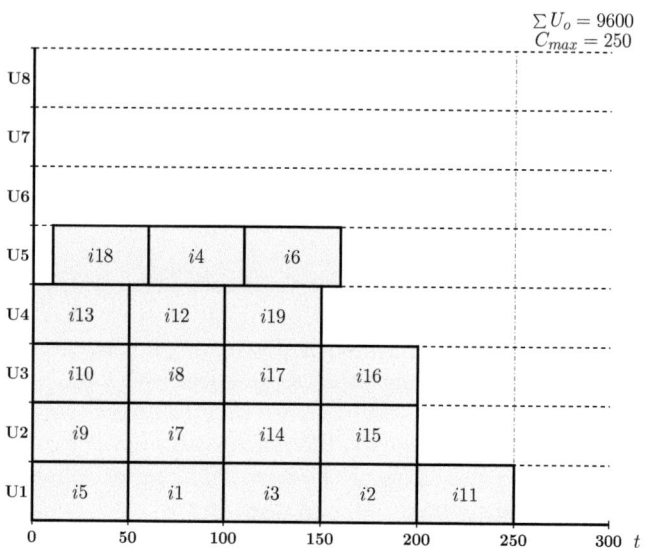

(a) Optimized truck schedule

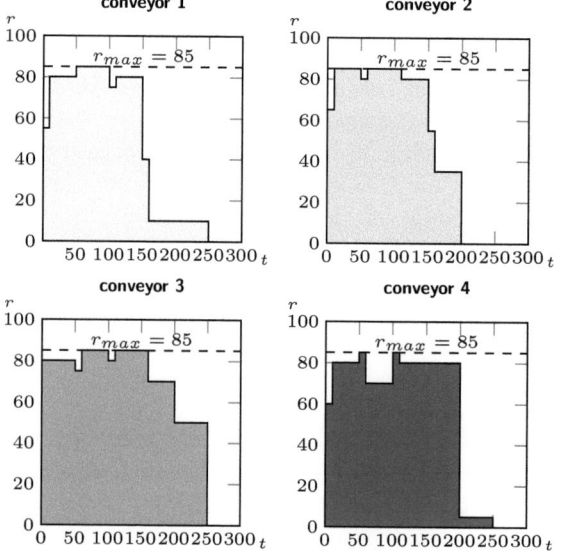

(b) Optimized conveyor utilization

Figure 6.4.: Optimized schedule and conveyor utilization for the Fix-policy

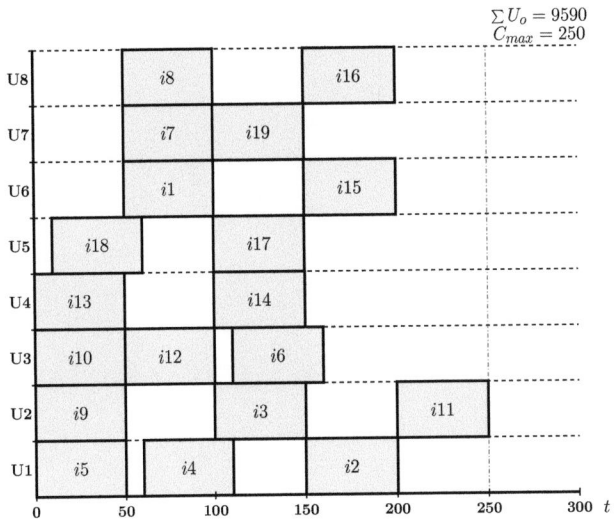

(a) Simulated truck schedule homogenized

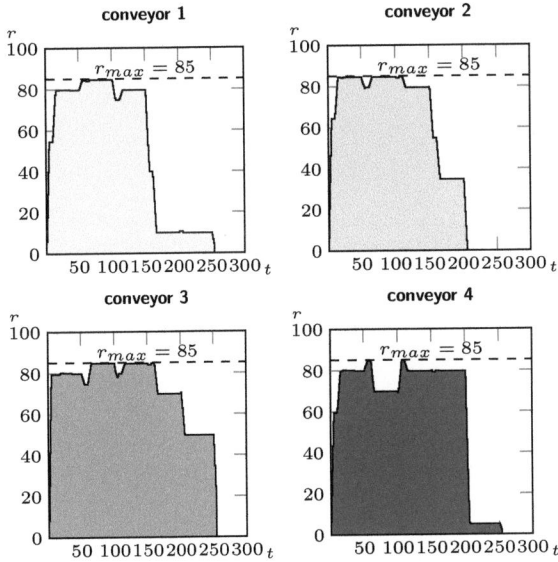

(b) Simulated conveyor utilization homogenized

Figure 6.5.: Simulated schedule and conveyor utilization for the *Fix*-policy with homogenized unloading sequences

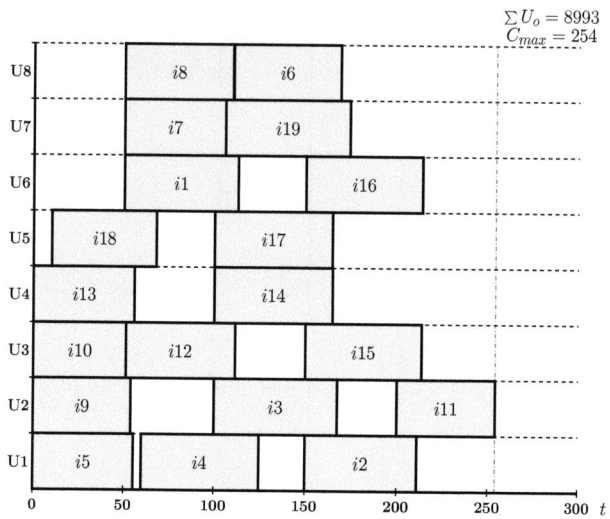

(a) Simulated truck schedule heterogeneous

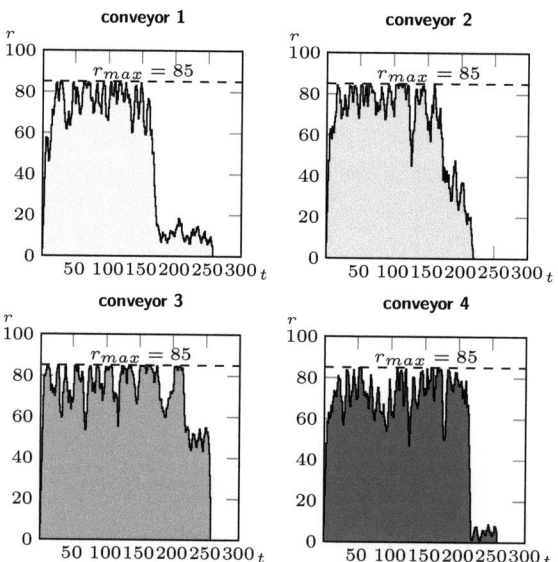

(b) Simulated conveyor utilization heterogeneous

Figure 6.6.: Simulated schedule and conveyor utilization for the *Fix*-policy with heterogeneous unloading sequences

of non-delayed parcels than when applying the FCFS scheduling policy $\sum_o U_o^{FCFS} = 7735$ as shown in Section 6.3.1 on page 120.
Applying the PHSP-LCC-flex model and the *Flex* scheduling policy with homogenized and heterogeneous unloading sequences to the example leads to the schedules and conveyor utilization shown in Figures 6.7, 6.8 and 6.9.

The *Flex* scheduling policy only uses the starting times calculated by the PHSP-LCC-flex even though the mathematical model formulation also determines the number of unloaded parcels that are unloaded in each period. Thus, the *Flex* scheduling policy does not utilize all the information provided by the solution of the mathematical model. Consequently, the makespan of $C_{max}^{opt} = 220$ and number of non-delayed parcels of $\sum_o U_o^{opt} = 10264$ resulting from applying the PHSP-LCC-flex model to the exemplary instance cannot be attained in the simulation model. Here, using the *Flex* scheduling policy leads to a makespan of $C_{max}^{hom} = 227$ and $\sum_o U_o^{hom} = 9573$ non-delayed parcels assuming homogenized unloading sequences. A closer look at the resulting schedules for the PHSP-LCC-flex in Figure 6.7a and the *Flex* scheduling policy in Figure 6.8a reveals that inbound trucks with a deliberately longer duration of the unloading process as calculated with the mathematical model such as $i3$ and $i15$ now have a shorter unloading duration in the simulation. This leads to congestion on the conveyors and delays for succeeding inbound trucks. The effect is even more pronounced for heterogeneous unloading patterns as random accumulations of parcels for individual conveyors increase the likelihood of congestion. This is reflected in a longer makespan of $C_{max}^{het} = 229$ and a decreased number of parcels arriving on time with $\sum_o U_o^{het} = 9311$. Generally, the number of non-delayed parcels is still larger when compared to both the *Fix* and FCFS scheduling policy. The Figures 6.10 and 6.11 show the respective schedules and conveyor utilization for the PHSP-LCC-flex and the *Flex*$^+$ scheduling policy.

The *Flex*$^+$ scheduling policy utilizes both the unloading speeds and the inbound truck starting times calculated by the PHSP-LCC-flex. For homogeneous unloading sequences, both the makespan of $C_{max}^{hom} = 225$ and the number of non-delayed parcels $\sum_o U_o^{hom} = 10045$ slightly deviates from the optimized value of $C_{max}^{opt} = 225$ and $\sum_o U_o^{opt} = 10264$, respectively. The unloading speeds the *Flex*$^+$ scheduling policy takes from the results of the mathematical model are highly dependent on the current state of the system with regard to the gate and conveyor

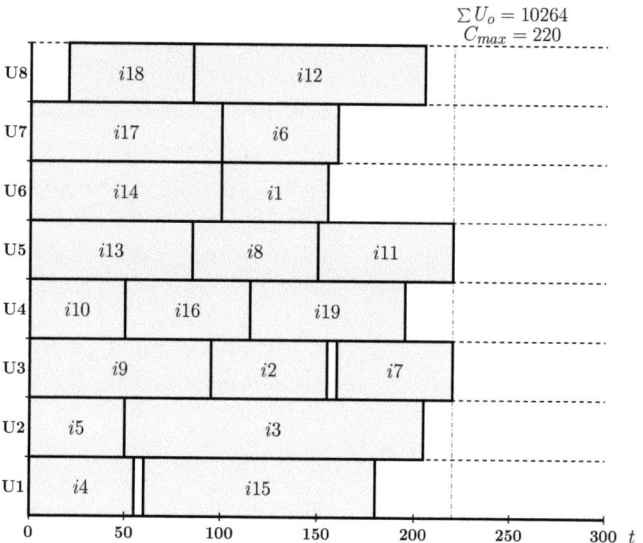

(a) Optimized schedule

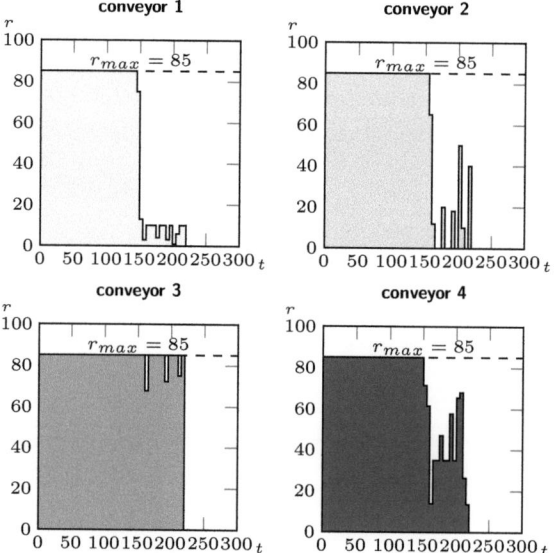

(b) Optimized conveyor utilization

Figure 6.7.: Optimized schedule and conveyor utilization for the *Flex-*
policy

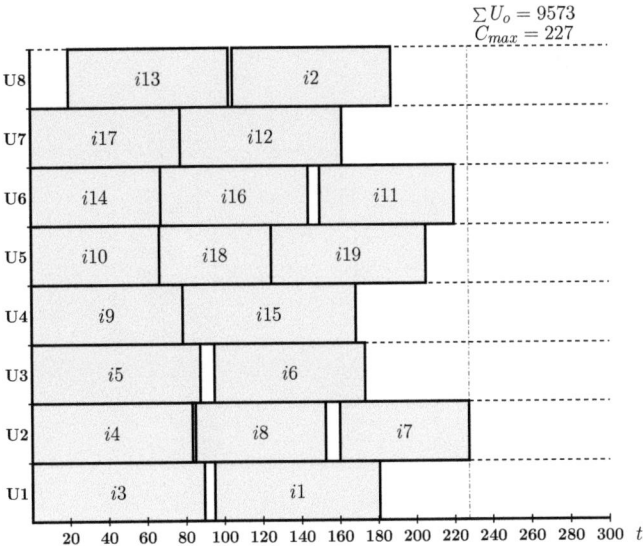

$\sum U_o = 9573$
$C_{max} = 227$

(a) Schedule homogeneous *Flex*-policy

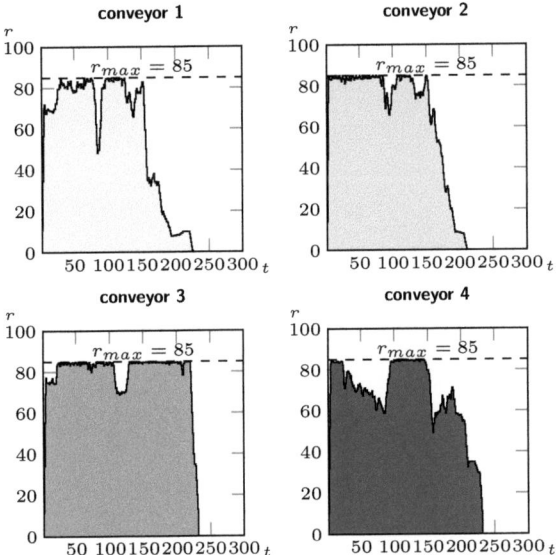

(b) Homogenized conveyor utilization

Figure 6.8.: Simulated schedule and conveyor utilization for the *Flex*-policy with homogenized unloading sequences

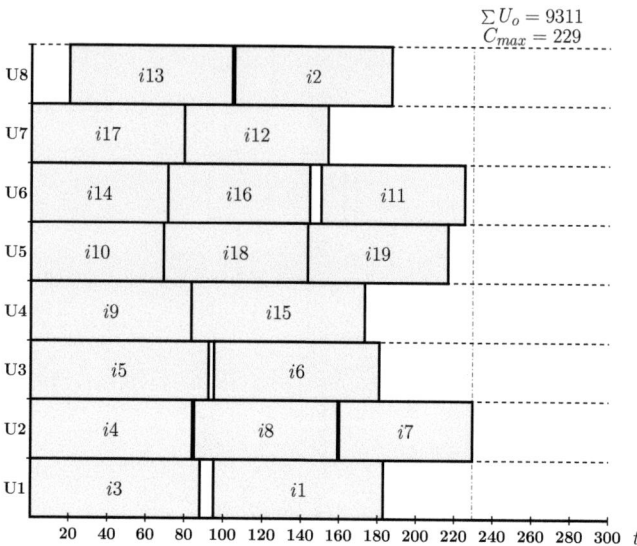

(a) Schedule heterogeneous *Flex*-policy

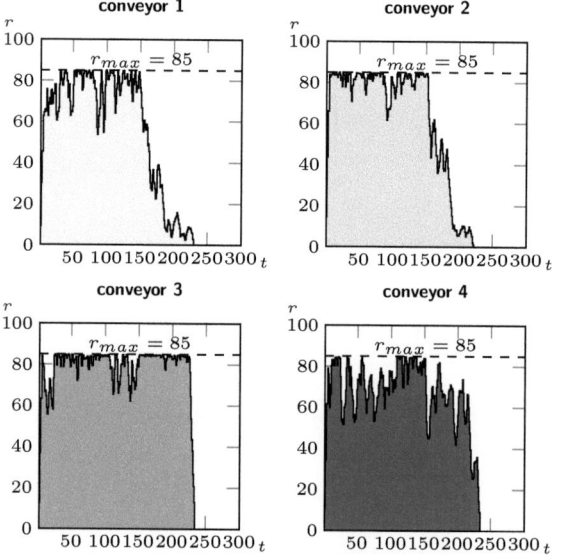

(b) Heterogeneous conveyor utilization

Figure 6.9.: Simulated schedule and conveyor utilization for the *Flex*-policy with heterogeneous unloading sequences

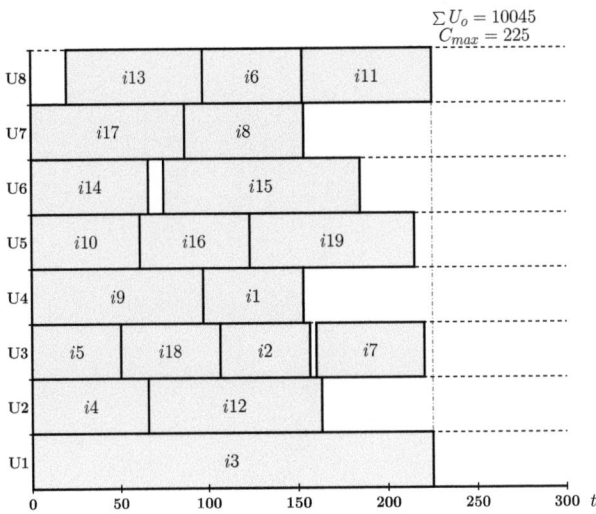

(a) Schedule homogenized $Flex^+$-policy

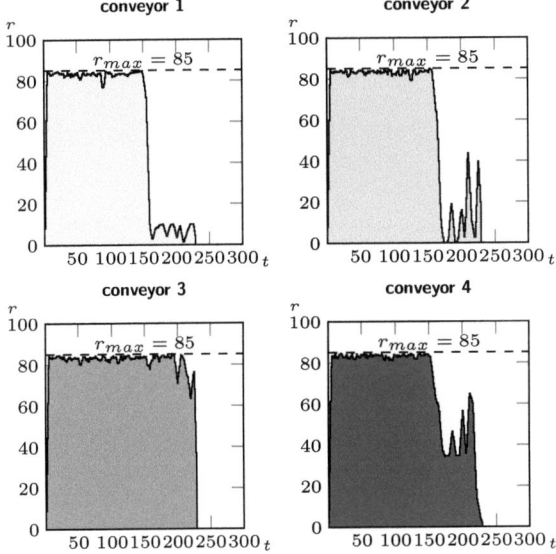

(b) Homogenized conveyor utilization

Figure 6.10.: Simulated schedule and conveyor utilization for the $Flex^+$-policy with homogenized unloading sequences

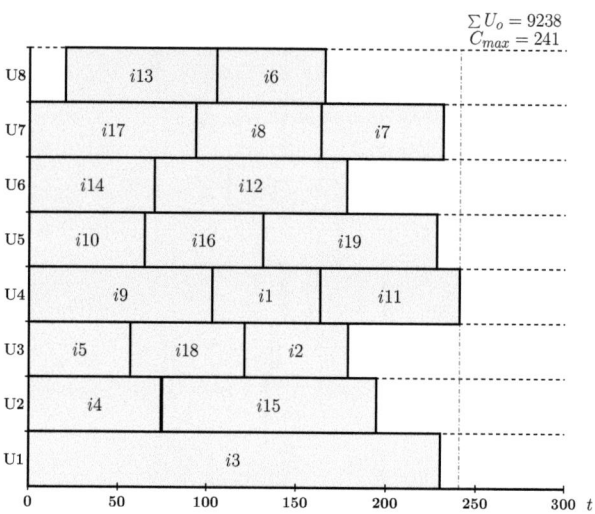

(a) Schedule heterogeneous $Flex^+$-policy

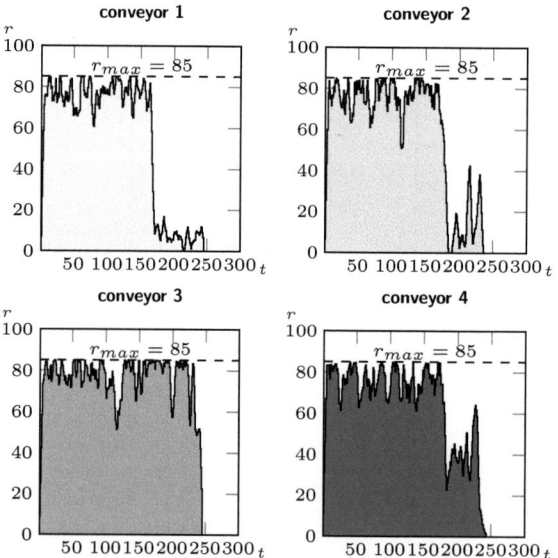

(b) Heterogeneous conveyor utilization

Figure 6.11.: Simulated schedule and conveyor utilization for the $Flex^+$-policy with heterogeneous unloading sequences

utilization and only directly applicable if the inbound truck schedule is executed as planned in the model. Smaller variations of the plan due to, e.g.,the discretization or small delays in the simulation model have implications on the state of the system and lead to a desynchronisation of the unloading speeds and the system state. Thus, even for homogenized unloading sequences, the results of the mathematical model cannot be replicated in the simulation. For heterogeneous unloading sequences the effect is even more pronounced and leads to a makespan of $C_{max}^{het} = 227$ and number of non-delayed parcels $\sum_o U_o^{het} = 9238$ for the shown exemplary randomized unloading sequences.

Lastly, Figures 6.12 and 6.13 show the respective schedules and conveyor utilization for the PHSP-LCC-flex and the $Flex^{prio}$ scheduling policy.

The $Flex^{prio}$ scheduling policy makes use of the inbound truck starting times calculated by the PHSP-LCC-flex and calculates priority values based on the unloading speeds determined by the model. With a makespan of $C_{max}^{hom} = 227$ the simulation results assuming homogeneous unloading sequences slightly deviate from the optimized value of $C_{max}^{opt} = 225$. Further, the number of non-delayed parcel $\sum_o U_o^{hom} = 9621$ is slightly higher than for the $Flex$ policy with $\sum_o U_o^{hom} = 9573$. Thus, the prioritization of trucks according to their intended number of unload parcels at a given point in time exhibits slight benefits for the given instance in the idealized setting assuming homogeneous unloading sequences. For heterogeneous unloading sequences, the resulting number of non-delayed parcels is again lower with $\sum_o U_o^{het} = 9295$ and the makespan is slightly higher with $C_{max}^{het} = 232$ compared to the results assuming homogeneous unloading sequences.

To conclude, the exemplary application of the different scheduling policies based on the results of mathematical models shows that even smaller deviations throughout the execution of a schedule can have a significant influence on the resulting makespan and number of delayed parcels in the simulation model. In this regard, randomized unloading sequences lead to major deviations with regard to the quality of the solution for all scheduling policies. Especially the $Flex^+$ policy is susceptible to deviations and appears to be the least robust. However, all scheduling policies constitute an improvement when compared to the FCFS scheduling policy. The applicability of scheduling policies is further investigated in a numeric study in the remainder of this chapter.

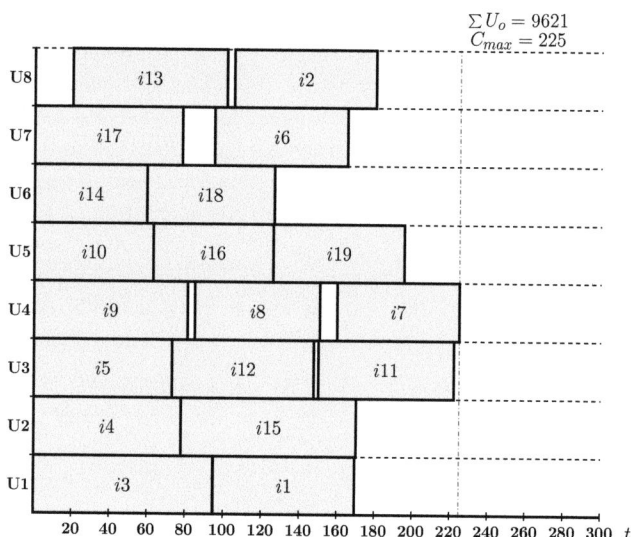

(a) Schedule homogenized $Flex^{prio}$-policy

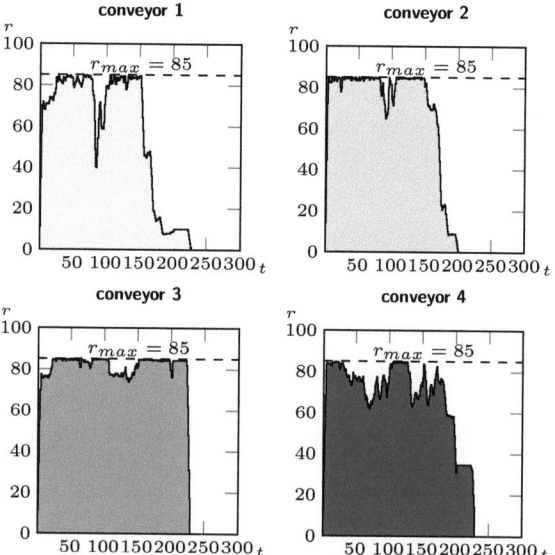

(b) Homogenized conveyor utilization

Figure 6.12.: Simulated schedule and conveyor utilization for the $Flex^{prio}$-policy with homogenized unloading sequences

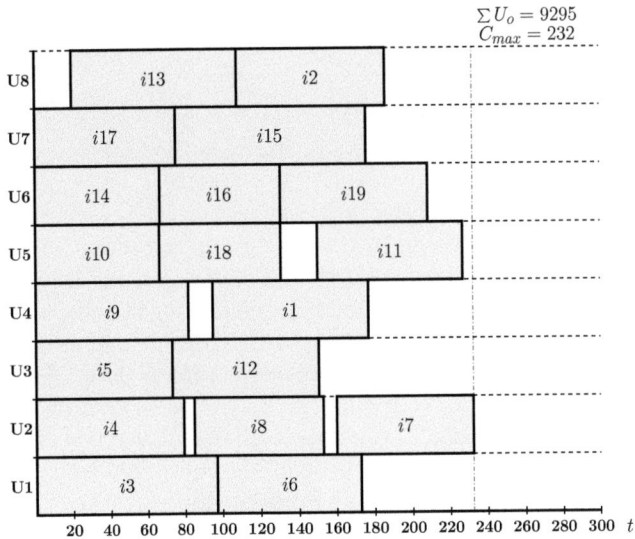

(a) Schedule heterogeneous $Flex^{prio}$-policy

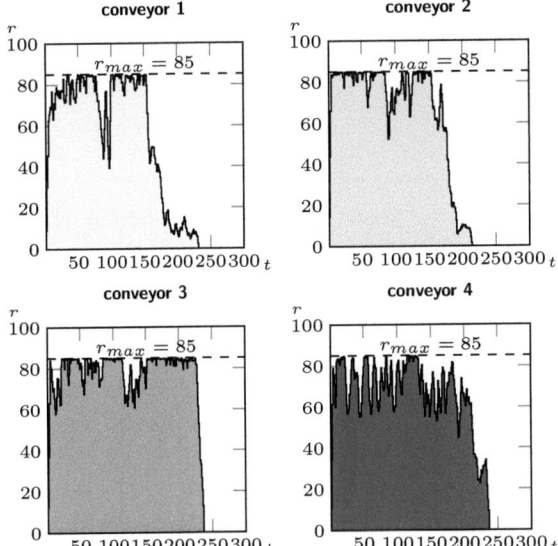

(b) Heterogeneous conveyor utilization

Figure 6.13.: Simulated schedule and conveyor utilization for the $Flex^{prio}$-policy with heterogeneous unloading sequences

6.4. Numerical analysis of the simulation model for the PHSP-LCC

6.4.1. Test design

The goal of the numerical study is to determine the broader applicability of optimized inbound schedules using the simulation model and expands on the preliminary view of the previous section. Thus, the simulation model is applied to the test instances introduced in Section 4.5.1 on page 65 to evaluate the performance of the schedules generated by the MIP-models under the assumption of uncertain unloading sequences. Both the results of the PHSP-LCC-fix and PHSP-LCC-flex in conjunction with the mentioned scheduling policies are considered. Here, the FCFS policy is again used as a reference. To render the results more tangible, the share of parcels arriving on time in relation to the total number of parcels is presented. For each instance and scheduling policy 100 simulation runs are conducted with respective random unloading sequences.

6.4.2. Numerical results

Table 6.3 shows the numeric results for the simulation study. Each line shows the average share of non-delayed parcels over all simulation runs for all instances with the given values of the scarcity factors β and σ. These instances include all combinations of the parameters μ and α for five replications, respectively. Thus, each row shows the averages for 100 simulation runs for each of the $3 \cdot 3 \cdot 5 = 45$ instances with the given values for σ and β. The results are presented for the FCFS policy (FCFS), for truck schedules generated with the PHSP-LCC-fix and the scheduling policy that applies the generated starting times (Fix). Further, the results using the starting times generated with the PHSP-LCC-flex ($Flex$) and in case both the starting times and unloading speeds from the PHSP-LCC-flex ($Flex^+$) are employed.

In Table 6.3 we can observe an increase of the share of non-delayed parcels by an average of 1.3 percentage points both for the small instances and large instances when employing the $Flex$ policy compared to the reference values of the FCFS policy. Further, the $Flex^+$ policy only shows smaller improvements with regard to the number of parcels without delay when compared to the results of the $Flex$ policy on average. Generally,

Table 6.3.: Percentage of non-delayed parcels for the scheduling policies

size	σ	β	FCFS	Fix	Flex	Flex$^+$	Flex^{prio}
	0.9	0.9	70.7	70.9	71.1	72.2	72.5
	1.0	0.9	77.4	77.5	77.7	79.2	79.7
	1.1	0.9	82.4	82.6	82.8	84.1	85.0
	0.9	1.0	72.7	72.9	73.2	72.7	72.9
small	1.0	1.0	79.3	79.5	79.7	81.0	81.3
	1.1	1.0	86.4	86.6	86.8	87.3	87.6
	0.9	1.1	72.9	73.2	73.4	72.2	72.5
	1.0	1.1	80.6	80.8	81.0	81.6	81.9
	1.1	1.1	86.8	86.9	87.1	87.5	87.7
	$\varnothing$		**78.8**	**79.0**	**79.2**	**79.7**	**80.1**
	0.9	0.9	71.3	71.6	71.8	72.8	73.2
	1.0	0.9	77.8	78.0	78.3	78.7	79.5
	1.1	0.9	82.8	83.0	83.2	82.3	83.4
	0.9	1.0	72.4	72.6	72.9	73.5	73.8
large	1.0	1.0	78.6	78.9	79.1	80.1	80.7
	1.1	1.0	84.6	84.8	85.0	85.5	86.1
	0.9	1.1	73.5	73.8	74.0	73.8	74.2
	1.0	1.1	81.0	81.3	81.6	82.0	82.3
	1.1	1.1	88.4	88.7	88.9	88.4	88.7
	$\varnothing$		**78.9**	**79.2**	**79.4**	**79.7**	**80.2**

the results confirm the observations of Section 6.3 with regard to the applicability of optimized truck schedules as their full potential is limited by the desynchronization effects of heterogeneous unloading sequences. As a whole, applying the *Flex*, *Flex$^+$* and *Flex^{prio}* policy does however increase the number of non-delayed parcels in comparison to the FCFS policy. It is further notable that the *Fix* policy only leads to a minor increase regarding the share of non-delayed parcels for some instances compared to the FCFS policy.

Figure 6.14 shows the results of the simulation experiments for instances with fixed values for α, μ, σ and β separately to allow for deeper insights concerning the performance of each scheduling policy in the specific circumstances. Each bar illustrates the average improvement for a specific scheduling policy compared to the FCFS scheduling policy for both the smaller and larger instances. Each diagram thus represents the results of 135 instances each.

The results show that especially for low values of α and thus low heterogeneity concerning the parcel destinations the *Flex*, *Flex$^+$* and *Flex^{prio}*

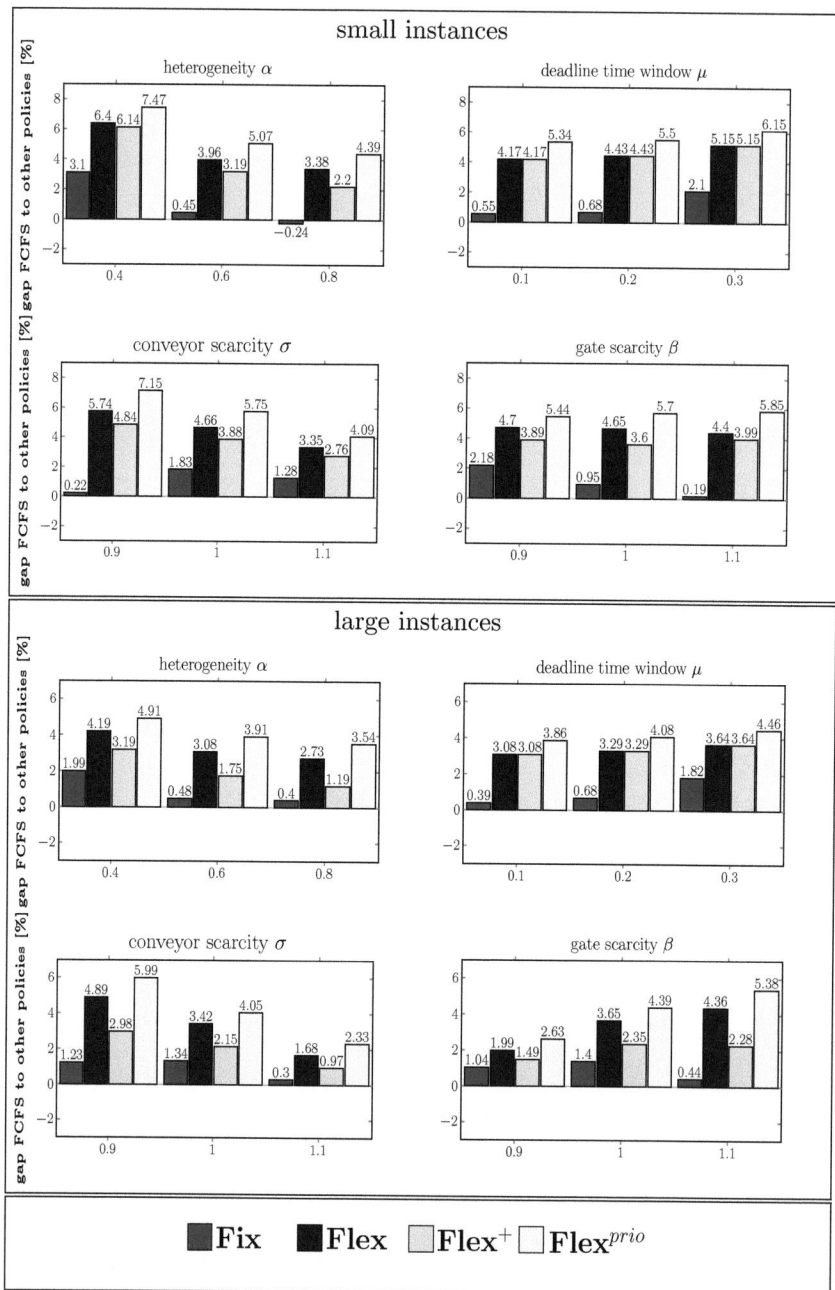

Figure 6.14.: Comparison FCFS and optimized schedules

policy perform well. Instances with low values of α reflect operational settings where parcels are concentrated for specific destinations. Hence, parcels unloaded from the inbound trucks are also designated mainly for the same conveyors. The unloading sequence thus mostly comprises of parcels for the same conveyors. Accordingly, the resulting randomized unloading sequences resemble each other more closely between the individual simulation runs and random accumulations for parcels for specific conveyors are less frequent. This leads to a diminished impact of the uncertain unloading sequences compared to instances with a higher degree of heterogeneity. We can observe that the *Flex*, *Flex*$^+$ and *Flex*^{prio} generate similar results for instances with higher values for β and lower values of σ reflecting particularly scarce conveyor and lose gate capacities. Especially for higher values σ, the improvement is less pronounced. Since the approach of controllable unloading speeds can only lead to improvements if the conveyor capacities are actually scarce, this is to be expected. The deadline distribution μ only has a minor influence on the performance of the *Flex*, *Flex*$^+$ and *Flex1prio* policy as the results are similar for all values of μ.

Concerning the *Fix* policy, the results show that it sometimes leads to a lower number of non-delayed parcels or only minor improvements compared to the FCFS-policy. We observe large deviations for instances with scarce conveyor capacities ($\sigma = 0.9$) and high levels of parcel heterogeneity ($\alpha = 0.8$), i.e., if many parcels are designated for only a few outbound gates. We can attribute these deviations to the non-usage of available conveyor capacities. These available capacities are not utilized since the PHSP-LCC-fix forbids the concurrent unloading of certain sets of inbound trucks that would together exceed the capacity of an individual conveyor. Hence, excluding flexibility in truck schedules also leads to suboptimal results in the simulation.

The influence of the instance size on the performance of the scheduling policies is similar as both instance sizes show the same general tendencies if all other instance parameters are identical. For smaller instances, the extent of the deviations is larger, though.

To conclude, the numeric study shows that the potentials of controllable unloading speeds cannot be fully exploited in circumstances with uncertain and heterogeneous unloading sequences if we apply the scheduling policies that have been outlined. The main reasons are the desynchronization of unloading speeds between model and application and deviations from planned starting times due to small delays. Utilizing scheduling policies that use the starting times generated by the PHSP-LCC-flex model does however lead to an increase of non-delayed parcels compared to the FCFS scheduling policy for all instances and especially when conveyor capacities are scarce and for a low heterogeneity of parcel destinations. Remarkably, even when we do not explicitly utilize the calculated unloading speeds by the model and only use the starting times, improvements are observable. Further, directly applying the calculated unloading speeds of the PHSP-LCC-flex model mostly leads to inferior results compared to only using the calculated starting times as these unloading speeds are highly dependant on the current system state and even small delays lead to desynchronization. However, using the calculated unloading speeds as part of a priority rule is generally beneficial.

7. Conclusion

7.1. Summary

This dissertation investigated the truck scheduling problem at parcel hubs with the explicit consideration of internal transportation via conveyor belts with limited capacities and the option of controlling unloading speeds. The novel problem setting was first contextualized in the broader field of designing and operating parcel hubs in general and more specific with regard to the truck scheduling problem at parcel hubs. The characteristics of parcel transport and handling at parcel hubs as well as relevant planning problems were outlined. Further, truck scheduling problems at parcel hubs were classified and an overview of the relevant literature was presented.

The problem setting was formalized as a mixed-integer program and designated as PHSP-LCC-fix for the case of fixed unloading speeds and PHSP-LCC-flex for the assumption of controllable unloading speeds. Both a time-based and an interval-based formulation were presented and proven to be NP-hard with regard to their computational complexity. An instance generation scheme was developed and utilized in a numeric study to empirically assess the performance of the time-based and interval-based formulation as well as the theoretical potentials of allowing controllable unloading speeds with regard to the number of non-delayed parcels. The study showed that allowing controllable unloading speeds is especially valuable for operational settings where the conveyor capacity constitutes the bottleneck of the system.

Since the problem is NP-hard but solutions have to be generated within a short time frame in a practical setting, a heuristic solution method, namely a genetic algorithm, was developed. For the genetic algorithm, solutions were represented as individuals in random-key representation and a biased elitist evolutionary strategy was applied. Individuals were decoded and evaluated with a decoding scheme that translates individuals in random-key representation to truck schedules. An LP-based improvement scheme was applied to enhance the solution quality. A numeric study utilizing the same instances as in the numeric analysis of the mathematical models was devised to evaluate the performance of the genetic algorithm in different variants. The results showed that the algorithm can find adequate solutions within a short frame and outperforms the standard solver Gurobi for short time limits.

To investigate the practical applicability of truck schedules generated with the PHSP-LCC-fix and PHSP-LCC-flex, a simulation model was developed. The simulation model allowed analyzing the impact of uncertainty regarding parcel unloading sequences on the performance of optimized truck schedules. To implement and evaluate optimized truck schedules with the simulation model, four scheduling policies were developed. The application of those scheduling policies was tested in a numeric study with the instances used for evaluation of the mathematical models and genetic algorithm. The results showed that the theoretical potentials of controllable unloading speeds cannot be fully exploited in a more practical setting. However, applying optimized truck schedules with the corresponding scheduling policies leads to significant improvements compared to conventional dispatching rules such as FCFS.

7.2. Outlook

The PHSP-LCC studied in this work formalizes a problem setting that explicitly considers internal transport capacities of parcel hubs and investigates ways to efficiently utilize those capacities. Those internal transport capacities are assumed to be distinct conveyor belts that directly connect inbound and outbound gates. In some practical settings of the postal service industry, those conveyor belts are organized in loop configuration and parcels remain on the conveyors until they are loaded onto the outbound gates.[1] It would be interesting to investigate how flexibility in the unloading process of inbound trucks would influence the performance of these or similar systems.

Another worthwhile addition to the setting would be to consider the number of tardy outbound *trucks* instead of individual *parcels* as the optimization criterion. Since tardy parcels are forwarded using additional vehicles as illustrated in Chapter 2, minimizing the number of additionally needed vehicles rather than parcels seems reasonable if using these

---

[1]Boysen et al. (2017, p. 724).

additional vehicles is costly.

One basic assumption concerning controllable unloading speeds is that we can chose the unloading speed freely but are limited by the maximum (standard) unloading speed. The practical background to flexible unloading speeds is that we assign workers to the unloading process of individual inbound trucks and decrease the unloading speed by withdrawing workers and assigning them to other inbound trucks.[2] This process of assigning workers is only approximated in the PHSP-LCC-flex and a thorough investigation on the detailed interaction of unloading speeds and the needed amount of workers as well as possible consequences on tactical staffing or shift scheduling problems and other related planning problems seems interesting.

Concerning uncertainty in the planning problem, the simulation model was used to address randomized unloading sequences. However, other stochastic influences such as inherent variations in the unloading times due to the size and dimension of the parcels, uncertain arrival times or conveyor failures also influence the truck scheduling problem in a practical setting. Addressing these uncertainties and their impact on the applicability of controllable unloading speeds as part of a scenario analysis could be interesting.

With regard to solving the problem heuristically, a genetic algorithm was proposed and investigated. However, the random-key representation employed in the algorithm does not necessarily include all feasible solutions. Thus, it potentially excludes the optimal solution as intentional delays for the unloading process of individual inbound trucks are not allowed. To allow for intentional delays, the representation could be extended by including a vector referencing the permitted delay for each inbound truck. Such a representation has already been used to solve the resource constrained multi-project scheduling problem as described by Mendes et al. (2009). To further enhance the performance of the genetic algorithm presented in this work, such an extension of the representation seems promising.

Another way to improve the performance of the genetic algorithm further might be to take a closer look at the algorithm parameters such as population size, selection probabilities and others. The values of these parameters often have a significant influence on the performance of the algorithm and have a varying impact for different instances.[3] Adequate

---

[2]Tadumadze et al. (2019).

[3]Hutter et al. (2011, p. 407).

values for the algorithm parameters can either be found by *parameter tuning* before or by *parameter control* throughout the execution of the algorithm.[4] Here, especially the field of machine learning provides efficient tools to help finding suitable algorithm parameters for each individual instance.[5]

Generally, this research on the truck scheduling problem at parcel hubs with limited conveyor capacities shows the value of flexibility in this problem setting. Similar problem settings appear in other industries such as baggage transport on conveyors at airports.[6] Thus, it might also be beneficial to incorporate the option of flexibility for other related problem settings that include shared resources.

---

[4]Eiben et al. (1999, p. 124).
[5]Karimi-Mamaghan et al. (2022, p. 396).
[6]Abdelghany et al. (2006).

Bibliography

Abdelghany, A., K. Abdelghany, and R. Narasimhan (2006). "Scheduling baggage-handling facilities in congested airports". In: *Journal of Air Transport Management* 12.2, pp. 76–81.

Agustina, D., C. Lee, and R. Piplani (2010). "A review: Mathematical models for cross docking planning". In: *International Journal of Engineering Business Management* 2.2, pp. 47–54.

Aickelin, U. and A. Adewunmi (2006). "Simulation optimization of the crossdock door assignment problem". In: *UK Operational Research Society Simulation Workshop 2006 (SW 2006), Leamington Spa, UK 2006*.

Alpan, G., R. Larbi, and B. Penz (2011). "A bounded dynamic programming approach to schedule operations in a cross docking platform". In: *Computers & Industrial Engineering* 60.3, pp. 385–396.

Alvarez-Perez, G., J. González-Velarde, and J. W. Fowler (2009). "Cross-docking—Just in Time scheduling: an alternative solution approach". In: *Journal of the Operational Research Society* 60.4, pp. 554–564.

Amaran, S., N. V. Sahinidis, B. Sharda, and S. J. Bury (2016). "Simulation optimization: a review of algorithms and applications". In: *Annals of Operations Research* 240.1, pp. 351–380.

Andradóttir, S. (1998). "A review of simulation optimization techniques". In: *1998 Winter Simulation Conference. Proceedings (Cat. No. 98CH36274)*. Vol. 1. IEEE, pp. 151–158.

Apex Insight (2021). *Global Parcel Delivery Market Insight Report 2021*. URL: https://apex-insight.com/product/global-parcel-delivery-market/ (visited on 09/23/2021).

Apte, U. M. and S. Viswanathan (2000). "Effective cross docking for improving distribution efficiencies". In: *International Journal of Logistics* 3.3, pp. 291–302.

Arabani, A. B., M. Zandieh, and S. F. Ghomi (2012). "A cross-docking scheduling problem with sub-population multi-objective algorithms". In: *The International Journal of Advanced Manufacturing Technology* 58.5, pp. 741–761.

Ardakani, A. A. and J. Fei (2020). "A systematic literature review on uncertainties in cross-docking operations". In: *Modern Supply Chain Research and Applications*.

Bachelet, B. and L. Yon (2007). "Model enhancement: Improving theoretical optimization with simulation". In: *Simulation Modelling Practice and Theory* 15.6, pp. 703–715.

Banks, J. (2003). "Discrete Event Simulation". In: *Encyclopedia of Information Systems*. Ed. by H. Bidgoli. New York: Elsevier, pp. 663–671.

Bányai, T. et al. (2012). "Direct shipment vs. cross docking". In: *Advanced Logistic Systems* 6.1, pp. 83–88.

Bartholdi, J. J. and K. R. Gue (2004). "The best shape for a crossdock". In: *Transportation Science* 38.2, pp. 235–244.

Bean, J. C. (1994). "Genetic algorithms and random keys for sequencing and optimization". In: *ORSA Journal on Computing* 6.2, pp. 154–160.

Berghman, L., C. Briand, R. Leus, and P. Lopez (2015). "The truck scheduling problem at crossdocking terminals-exclusive versus mixed mode". In: *4th International Conference on Operations Research and Enterprise Systems (ICORES 2015)*, pp–247.

Bermudez, R., M. H. Cole, and M.-B. T. Center (2001). *Genetic Algorithm Approach to Door Assignments in Breakbulk Terminals*. Tech. rep.

Besse, A. (2018). *Produktivitätssteigerung von Cross-Docking-Centern mit RFID*. Springer.

Bjelić, N., D. Popović, and B. Ratković (2013). "Genetic algorithm approach for solving truck scheduling problem with time robustness". In: *Proceedings of the 1st Logistics International Conference LOGIC*.

Bodnar, P., R. de Koster, and K. Azadeh (2017). "Scheduling trucks in a cross-dock with mixed service mode dock doors". In: *Transportation Science* 51.1, pp. 112–131.

Boysen, N. (2010). "Truck scheduling at zero-inventory cross docking terminals". In: *Computers & Operations Research* 37.1, pp. 32–41.

Boysen, N., D. Briskorn, and M. Tschöke (2013). "Truck scheduling in cross-docking terminals with fixed outbound departures". In: *OR Spectrum* 35.2, pp. 479–504.

Boysen, N., S. Fedtke, and F. Weidinger (2017). "Truck scheduling in the postal service industry". In: *Transportation Science* 51.2, pp. 723–736.

Boysen, N. and M. Fliedner (2010). "Cross dock scheduling: Classification, literature review and research agenda". In: *Omega* 38.6, pp. 413–422.

Boysen, N., M. Fliedner, and A. Scholl (2010). "Scheduling inbound and outbound trucks at cross docking terminals". In: *OR spectrum* 32.1, pp. 135–161.

Bugow, S. and C. Kellenbrink (2023). "The parcel hub scheduling problem with limited conveyor capacity and controllable unloading speeds". In: *OR Spectrum*, pp. 1–33.

Buijs, P., H. W. Danhof, and J. C. Wortmann (2016). "Just-in-Time Retail Distribution: A Systems Perspective on Cross-Docking". In: *Journal of Business Logistics* 37.3, pp. 213–230.

Buijs, P., I. F. Vis, and H. J. Carlo (2014). "Synchronization in cross-docking networks: A research classification and framework". In: *European Journal of Operational Research* 239.3, pp. 593–608.

Carlo, H. J. and Y. A. Bozer (2011). "Analysis of optimum shape and door assignment problems in rectangular unit-load crossdocks". In: *International Journal of Logistics Research and Applications* 14.3, pp. 149–163.

Chen, F. and C.-Y. Lee (2009). "Minimizing the makespan in a two-machine cross-docking flow shop problem". In: *European Journal of Operational Research* 193.1, pp. 59–72.

Chen, J. C., T.-L. Chen, T.-C. Ou, and Y.-H. Lee (2019). "Adaptive genetic algorithm for parcel hub scheduling problem with shortcuts in closed-loop sortation system". In: *Computers & Industrial Engineering* 138, 106114.

Cheng, T., Z. Chen, and C.-L. Li (1996). "Parallel-machine scheduling with controllable processing times". In: *IIE Transactions* 28.2, pp. 177–180.

Clausen, U., D. Diekmann, J. Baudach, J. Kaffka, and M. Pöting (2015). "Improving parcel transshipment operations-impact of different objective functions in a combined simulation and optimization approach". In: *2015 Winter Simulation Conference (WSC)*. IEEE, pp. 1924–1935.

Clausen, U., D. Diekmann, M. Pöting, and C. Schumacher (2017). "Operating parcel transshipment terminals: a combined simulation and optimization approach". In: *Journal of Simulation* 11.1, pp. 2–10.

Clausen, U., I. Goedicke, L. Mest, and S. Wohlgemuth (2012). "Combining simulation and optimization to improve LTL traffic". In: *Procedia-Social and Behavioral Sciences* 48, pp. 1993–2002.

Corsten, H., F. Becker, and H. Salewski (2020). "Integrating truck and workforce scheduling in a cross-dock: analysis of different workforce coordination policies". In: *Journal of Business Economics* 90.2, pp. 207–237.

Cox, D. A. and M. D. Rossetti (2017). "Simulation modeling of alternative staffing and task prioritization in manual post-distribution cross docking facilities". In: *2017 Winter Simulation Conference (WSC)*. IEEE, pp. 3447–3458.

Darwin, C. (1859). *On the Origin of Species by Means of Natural Selection. or the Preservation of Favored Races in the Struggle for Life*. London: Murray.

Davoudpour, H., P. Hooshangi-Tabrizi, and P. Hoseinpour (2012). "A genetic algorithm for truck scheduling in cross docking systems". In: *Journal of American Science* 8.2, pp. 96–99.

Eiben, Á. E., R. Hinterding, and Z. Michalewicz (1999). "Parameter control in evolutionary algorithms". In: *IEEE Transactions on Evolutionary Computation* 3.2, pp. 124–141.

eMarketer (2022). *Global Ecommerce Forecast 2022*. URL: https://www.emarketer.com/content/global-ecommerce-forecast-2022 (visited on 03/31/2022).

Emmons, H. (1969). "One-machine sequencing to minimize certain functions of job tardiness". In: *Operations Research* 17.4, pp. 701–715.

Erickson, J. P., J. H. Anderson, and B. C. Ward (2014). "Fair lateness scheduling: Reducing maximum lateness in G-EDF-like scheduling". In: *Real-Time Systems* 50.1, pp. 5–47.

Fedtke, S. and N. Boysen (2017). "Layout planning of sortation conveyors in parcel distribution centers". In: *Transportation Science* 51.1, pp. 3–18.

Fu, M. C. (2002). "Optimization for simulation: Theory vs. practice". In: *INFORMS Journal on Computing* 14.3, pp. 192–215.

Gambardella, L. M., A. E. Rizzoli, and M. Zaffalon (1998). "Simulation and planning of an intermodal container terminal". In: *Simulation* 71.2, pp. 107–116.

Gelareh, S., F. Glover, O. Guemri, S. Hanafi, P. Nduwayo, and R. Todosijević (2020). "A comparative study of formulations for a cross-dock door assignment problem". In: *Omega* 91, 102015.

Glover, F. W. and G. A. Kochenberger (2006). *Handbook of metaheuristics*. Vol. 57. Springer Science & Business Media.

Goldberg, D. E. (1989). *Genetic Algorithms in Search, Optimization and Machine Learning*. 1st. USA: Addison-Wesley Longman Publishing Co., Inc.

Golias, M. M., G. K. Saharidis, M. Boile, and S. Theofanis (2012). "Scheduling of inbound trucks at a cross-docking facility: Bi-objective vs bi-level modeling approaches". In: *International Journal of Information Systems and Supply Chain Management (IJISSCM)* 5.1, pp. 20–37.

Golias, M. M., G. K. Saharidis, S. Ivey, and H. E. Haralambides (2013). "Advances in truck scheduling at a cross dock facility". In: *International Journal of Information Systems and Supply Chain Management (IJISSCM)* 6.3, pp. 40–62.

Gonçalves, J. F. and M. G. Resende (2011). "Biased random-key genetic algorithms for combinatorial optimization". In: *Journal of Heuristics* 17.5, pp. 487–525.

Graham, R. L., E. L. Lawler, J. K. Lenstra, and A. R. Kan (1979). "Optimization and approximation in deterministic sequencing and scheduling: a survey". In: *Annals of discrete mathematics*. Vol. 5. Elsevier, pp. 287–326.

Gue, K. R. (1999). "The effects of trailer scheduling on the layout of freight terminals". In: *Transportation Science* 33.4, pp. 419–428.

Guo, Y., Z.-R. Chen, Y.-L. Ruan, and J. Zhang (2012). "Application of NSGA-II with local search to multi-dock cross-docking sheduling problem". In: *2012 IEEE International Conference on Systems, Man, and Cybernetics (SMC)*. IEEE, pp. 779–784.

Haneyah, S., J. M. Schutten, and K. Fikse (2014). "Throughput maximization of parcel sorter systems by scheduling inbound containers". In: *Efficiency and innovation in logistics*. Springer, pp. 147–159.

Hauser, K. (2002). "Simulation and optimization of a crossdocking operation in a just-in-time environment". PhD thesis.

Holland, J. H. (1975). *Adaptation in natural and artificial systems: an introductory analysis with applications to biology, control, and artificial intelligence*. U Michigan Press.

Hutter, F., H. H. Hoos, and K. Leyton-Brown (2011). "Sequential model-based optimization for general algorithm configuration". In: *International conference on learning and intelligent optimization*. Springer, pp. 507–523.

Ishfaq, R. and C. R. Sox (2012). "Design of intermodal logistics networks with hub delays". In: *European Journal of Operational Research* 220.3, pp. 629–641.

Jarrah, A. I., E. Johnson, and L. C. Neubert (2009). "Large-scale, less-than-truckload service network design". In: *Operations Research* 57.3, pp. 609–625.

Joo, C. M. and B. S. Kim (2013). "Scheduling compound trucks in multi-door cross-docking terminals". In: *The International Journal of Advanced Manufacturing Technology* 64.5-8, pp. 977–988.

Karimi-Mamaghan, M., M. Mohammadi, P. Meyer, A. M. Karimi-Mamaghan, and E.-G. Talbi (2022). "Machine Learning at the service of Metaheuristics for solving Combinatorial Optimization Problems: A state-of-the-art". In: *European Journal of Operational Research* 296.2, pp. 393–422.

Karnon, J., J. Stahl, A. Brennan, J. J. Caro, J. Mar, and J. Möller (2012). "Modeling using discrete event simulation: a report of the ISPOR-SMDM Modeling Good Research Practices Task Force–4". In: *Medical decision making* 32.5, pp. 701–711.

Kolen, A. W., J. K. Lenstra, C. H. Papadimitriou, and F. C. Spieksma (2007). "Interval scheduling: A survey". In: *Naval Research Logistics (NRL)* 54.5, pp. 530–543.

Kolisch, R. (1996). "Serial and parallel resource-constrained project scheduling methods revisited: Theory and computation". In: *European Journal of Operational Research* 90.2, pp. 320–333.

Koné, O., C. Artigues, P. Lopez, and M. Mongeau (2011). "Event-based MILP models for resource-constrained project scheduling problems". In: *Computers & Operations Research* 38.1, pp. 3–13.

Konur, D. and M. M. Golias (2013). "Cost-stable truck scheduling at a cross-dock facility with unknown truck arrivals: A meta-heuristic approach". In: *Transportation Research Part E: Logistics and Transportation Review* 49.1, pp. 71–91.

Koza, J. R. (1995). "Survey of genetic algorithms and genetic programming". In: *Proceedings of WESCON'95*. IEEE, pp. 589–594.

Ladier, A.-L. (2014). "Scheduling cross-docking operations: Integration of operational uncertainties and resource capacities". PhD thesis. Université de Grenoble.

Ladier, A.-L. and G. Alpan (2015). "Integrating truck scheduling and employee rostering in a cross-docking platform-an iterative approach". In: *2015 International Conference on Industrial Engineering and Systems Management (IESM)*. IEEE, pp. 676–685.

– (2016a). "Cross-docking operations: Current research versus industry practice". In: *Omega* 62, pp. 145–162.

– (2016b). "Robust cross-dock scheduling with time windows". In: *Computers & Industrial Engineering* 99, pp. 16–28.

– (2018). "Crossdock truck scheduling with time windows: earliness, tardiness and storage policies". In: *Journal of Intelligent Manufacturing* 29.3, pp. 569–583.

Ladier, A.-L., G. Alpan, and A. G. Greenwood (2014a). "Robustness evaluation of an integer programming-based cross-docking schedule using discrete-event simulation". In: *IIE Annual Conference. Proceedings.* Institute of Industrial and Systems Engineers (IISE), pp. 587–596.

Ladier, A.-L., A. G. Greenwood, G. Alpan, and H. Hales (2014b). "Issues in the complementary use of simulation and optimization modeling". In: *Soumis à Operational Research Society Simulation Workshop.*

Lawler, E. L. (1977). "A "pseudopolynomial" algorithm for sequencing jobs to minimize total tardiness". In: *Annals of discrete Mathematics.* Vol. 1. Elsevier, pp. 331–342.

Lee, Y. H., J. W. Jung, and K. M. Lee (2006). "Vehicle routing scheduling for cross-docking in the supply chain". In: *Computers & Industrial Engineering* 51.2, pp. 247–256.

Ley, S. and S. Elfayoumy (2007). "Cross dock scheduling using genetic algorithms". In: *2007 International Symposium on Computational Intelligence in Robotics and Automation.* IEEE, pp. 416–420.

Li, Y., A. Lim, and B. Rodrigues (2004). "Crossdocking—JIT scheduling with time windows". In: *Journal of the Operational Research Society* 55.12, pp. 1342–1351.

Liao, T. W., P.-C. Chang, R. Kuo, and C.-J. Liao (2014). "A comparison of five hybrid metaheuristic algorithms for unrelated parallel-machine scheduling and inbound trucks sequencing in multi-door cross docking systems". In: *Applied Soft Computing* 21, pp. 180–193.

Lim, A., H. Ma, and Z. Miao (2006). "Truck dock assignment problem with time windows and capacity constraint in transshipment network through crossdocks". In: *International Conference on Computational Science and Its Applications.* Springer, pp. 688–697.

Liu, Y. and S. Takakuwa (2009). "Simulation-based personnel planning for materials handling at a cross-docking center under retail distribution environment". In: *Proceedings of the 2009 Winter Simulation Conference (WSC).* IEEE, pp. 2414–2425.

Maknoon, M., O. Koné, and P. Baptiste (2014). "A sequential priority-based heuristic for scheduling material handling in a satellite cross-dock". In: *Computers & Industrial Engineering* 72, pp. 43–49.

Maknoon, M., F. Soumis, and P. Baptiste (2016). "Optimizing transshipment workloads in less-than-truckload cross-docks". In: *International Journal of Production Economics* 179, pp. 90–100.

Maknoon, M., F. Soumis, and P. Baptiste (2017). "An integer programming approach to scheduling the transshipment of products at cross-docks in less-than-truckload industries". In: *Computers & Operations Research* 82, pp. 167–179.

Malve, S. and R. Uzsoy (2007). "A genetic algorithm for minimizing maximum lateness on parallel identical batch processing machines with dynamic job arrivals and incompatible job families". In: *Computers & Operations Research* 34.10, pp. 3016–3028.

McWilliams, D. L. (2005). "Simulation-based scheduling for parcel consolidation terminals: a comparison of iterative improvement and simulated annealing". In: *Proceedings of the Winter Simulation Conference, 2005.* IEEE, pp. 2087–2093.

– (2009a). "A dynamic load-balancing scheme for the parcel hub-scheduling problem". In: *Computers & Industrial Engineering* 57.3, pp. 958–962.

– (2009b). "Genetic-based scheduling to solve the parcel hub scheduling problem". In: *Computers & Industrial Engineering* 56.4, pp. 1607–1616.

McWilliams, D. L. and M. E. McBride (2013). "Exploring mathematical approximation for the time spans of transfer operations in parcel transshipment terminals". In: *Computers & Industrial Engineering* 64.1, pp. 342–356.

McWilliams, D. L., P. M. Stanfield, and C. D. Geiger (2005). "The parcel hub scheduling problem: A simulation-based solution approach". In: *Computers & Industrial Engineering* 49.3, pp. 393–412.

– (2008). "Minimizing the completion time of the transfer operations in a central parcel consolidation terminal with unequal-batch-size inbound trailers". In: *Computers & Industrial Engineering* 54.4, pp. 709–720.

Mendel, G. (1866). "Versuche über Pflanzenhybriden". In: *Verhandlungen des naturforschenden Vereins in Brünn* 4, pp. 3–47.

Mendes, J. J., J. F. Gonçalves, and M. G. Resende (2009). "A random key based genetic algorithm for the resource constrained project scheduling problem". In: *Computers & Operations research* 36.1, pp. 92–109.

Mohtashami, A. (2015). "Scheduling trucks in cross docking systems with temporary storage and repetitive pattern for shipping trucks". In: *Applied Soft Computing* 36, pp. 468–486.

Molavi, D., A. Shahmardan, and M. S. Sajadieh (2018). "Truck scheduling in a cross docking systems with fixed due dates and shipment sorting". In: *Computers & Industrial Engineering* 117, pp. 29–40.

Morganti, E., S. Seidel, C. Blanquart, L. Dablanc, and B. Lenz (2014). "The impact of e-commerce on final deliveries: alternative parcel delivery services in France and Germany". In: *Transportation Research Procedia* 4, pp. 178–190.

Mousavi, S. M. and B. Vahdani (2016). "Cross-docking location selection in distribution systems: a new intuitionistic fuzzy hierarchical decision model". In: *International Journal of Computational Intelligence Systems* 9.1, pp. 91–109.

Naber, A. and R. Kolisch (2014). "MIP models for resource-constrained project scheduling with flexible resource profiles". In: *European Journal of Operational Research* 239.2, pp. 335–348.

Ou, J., V. N. Hsu, and C.-L. Li (2010). "Scheduling truck arrivals at an air cargo terminal". In: *Production and Operations Management* 19.1, pp. 83–97.

Prasetyo, H., G. Fauza, Y. Amer, and S.-H. Lee (2015). "Survey on applications of biased-random key genetic algorithms for solving optimization problems". In: *2015 IEEE International Conference on Industrial Engineering and Engineering Management (IEEM)*. IEEE, pp. 863–870.

Rijal, A., M. Bijvank, and R. de Koster (2019). "Integrated scheduling and assignment of trucks at unit-load cross-dock terminals with mixed service mode dock doors". In: *European Journal of Operational Research* 278.3, pp. 752–771.

Rothlauf, F. (2011). *Design of modern heuristics: principles and application*. Springer Science & Business Media.

Rotta, G.-L., E. Cristina, and M. Becerra-Fernández (2017). "Cross-docking with vehicle routing problem. A state of art review". In: *Dyna* 84.200, pp. 271–280.

Safe, M., J. Carballido, I. Ponzoni, and N. Brignole (2004). "On stopping criteria for genetic algorithms". In: *Brazilian Symposium on Artificial Intelligence*. Springer, pp. 405–413.

Sathasivan, K. (2011). "Optimizing cross-dock operations under uncertainty". PhD thesis.

Savelsbergh, M. and T. Van Woensel (2016). "50th anniversary invited article—city logistics: Challenges and opportunities". In: *Transportation Science* 50.2, pp. 579–590.

Serrano, C., X. Delorme, and A. Dolgui (2017). "Scheduling of truck arrivals, truck departures and shop-floor operation in a cross-dock platform, based on trucks loading plans". In: *International Journal of Production Economics* 194, pp. 102–112.

Shabtay, D. and G. Steiner (2007). "A survey of scheduling with controllable processing times". In: *Discrete Applied Mathematics* 155.13, pp. 1643–1666.

Shahmardan, A. and M. S. Sajadieh (2020). "Truck scheduling in a multi-door cross-docking center with partial unloading–Reinforcement learning-based simulated annealing approaches". In: *Computers & Industrial Engineering* 139, p. 106134.

Shiguemoto, A. L., U. S. Cavalcante Netto, and G. H. S. Bauab (2014). "An efficient hybrid meta-heuristic for a cross-docking system with temporary storage". In: *International Journal of Production Research* 52.4, pp. 1231–1239.

Spears, W. M. and K. D. De Jong (1995). *On the virtues of parameterized uniform crossover.* Tech. rep. Naval Research Lab Washington DC.

Stephan, K. and N. Boysen (2011). "Cross-docking". In: *Journal of Management Control* 22.1, pp. 129–137.

Sung, C. S. and S. H. Song (2003). "Integrated service network design for a cross-docking supply chain network". In: *Journal of the Operational Research Society* 54.12, pp. 1283–1295.

Tadumadze, G., N. Boysen, S. Emde, and F. Weidinger (2019). "Integrated truck and workforce scheduling to accelerate the unloading of trucks". In: *European Journal of Operational Research* 278.1, pp. 343–362.

Tekin, E. and I. Sabuncuoglu (2004). "Simulation optimization: A comprehensive review on theory and applications". In: *IIE Transactions* 36.11, pp. 1067–1081.

Theophilus, O., M. A. Dulebenets, J. Pasha, O. F. Abioye, and M. Kavoosi (2019). "Truck scheduling at cross-docking terminals: a follow-up state-of-the-art review". In: *Sustainability* 11.19, 5245.

Thierens, D. and D. Goldberg (1994). "Elitist recombination: An integrated selection recombination GA". In: *Proceedings of the First IEEE Conference on Evolutionary Computation. IEEE World Congress on Computational Intelligence.* IEEE, pp. 508–512.

Tomassini, M. (1995). "A survey of genetic algorithms". In: *Annual Reviews of Computational Physics III*, pp. 87–118.

Tootkaleh, S. R., S. F. Ghomi, and M. S. Sajadieh (2016). "Cross dock scheduling with fixed outbound trucks departure times under substitution condition". In: *Computers & Industrial Engineering* 92, pp. 50–56.

Tripp, C. (2021). "Dienstleisternetze in der Distributionslogistik". In: *Distri- butions- und Handelslogistik.* Springer, pp. 359–421.

Vahdani, B. and M. Zandieh (2010). "Scheduling trucks in cross-docking systems: Robust meta-heuristics". In: *Computers & Industrial Engineering* 58.1, pp. 12–24.

Van Belle, J., P. Valckenaers, and D. Cattrysse (2012). "Cross-docking: State of the art". In: *Omega* 40.6, pp. 827–846.

Van den Akker, J., C. A. Hurkens, and M. W. Savelsbergh (2000). "Time-indexed formulations for machine scheduling problems: Column generation". In: *INFORMS Journal on Computing* 12.2, pp. 111–124.

Vepsalainen, A. P. and T. E. Morton (1987). "Priority rules for job shops with weighted tardiness costs". In: *Management Science* 33.8, pp. 1035–1047.

Vis, I. F. and K. J. Roodbergen (2008). "Positioning of goods in a cross-docking environment". In: *Computers & Industrial Engineering* 54.3, pp. 677–689.

Vogt, J. J. and W. J. Pienaar (2007). "The cross-dock: a new viewpoint on the definition and the design of the facility". In: *Southern African Business Review* 11.1, pp. 87–103.

Walha, F., S. Chaabane, A. Bekrar, and T. Loukil (2014). "The cross docking under uncertainty: State of the art". In: *2014 International Conference on Advanced Logistics and Transport (ICALT)*. IEEE, pp. 330–335.

Wang, J.-F. and A. Regan (2008). "Real-time trailer scheduling for crossdock operations". In: *Transportation Journal*, pp. 5–20.

Wolff, P., S. Emde, and H.-C. Pfohl (2021). "Internal resource requirements: The better performance metric for truck scheduling?" In: *Omega* 103, 102431.

Wu, Y., M. Dong, and D. Yang (2011). "Cross-docking centre operation optimization using simulation-based genetic algorithm". In: *Proceedings of the Institution of Mechanical Engineers, Part B: Journal of Engineering Manufacture* 225.7, pp. 1175–1187.

Yang, X.-S. (2010). *Nature-inspired metaheuristic algorithms*. Luniver press.

Yazdani, M., B. Naderi, and M. Mousakhani (2015). "A model and metaheuristic for truck scheduling in multi-door cross-dock problems". In: *Intelligent Automation & Soft Computing* 21.4, pp. 633–644.

Ye, Y., J.-f. Li, R. Y. Fung, K. Li, and H. Fu (2018). "Optimizing truck scheduling in a cross-docking system with preemption and unloading/loading sequence constraint". In: *2018 IEEE 15th International Conference on Networking, Sensing and Control (ICNSC)*. IEEE, pp. 1–6.

Yu, V. F., D. Sharma, and K. G. Murty (2008). "Door allocations to origins and destinations at less-than-truckload trucking terminals". In: *Journal of Industrial and Systems Engineering* 2.1, pp. 1–15.

Yu, W. and P. J. Egbelu (2008). "Scheduling of inbound and outbound trucks in cross docking systems with temporary storage". In: *European Journal of Operational Research* 184.1, pp. 377–396.

Zanakis, S. H. and J. R. Evans (1981). "Heuristic "optimization": Why, when, and how to use it". In: *Interfaces* 11.5, pp. 84–91.

Zenker, M. and N. Boysen (2017). "Dock sharing in cross-docking facilities of the postal service industry". In: *Journal of the Operational Research Society*, pp. 1–17.

Zouhaier, H. and L. B. Said (2017). "Robust scheduling of truck arrivals at a cross-docking platform". In: *Proceedings of the Australasian Computer Science Week Multiconference*, pp. 1–9.

Appendix

A. Events in the simulation model

A.1. Arriving inbound truck

At the arrival time $at_{i'}$ of an inbound truck i', the event $e = I$ *Arriving inbound truck* occurs. Some more sophisticated scheduling policies prescribe an earliest starting time. In case the starting time of the arriving inbound $start_i^*$ has not been reached yet, another *Arriving inbound truck* event is created for the starting time. If the planned earliest starting time has already been passed, the current position of the inbound truck pos_i is set to the parking lot and i is added to the set of currently parked inbound trucks $PA(t^c)$. If all gates $g, u \in G$ are currently occupied by other inbound trucks as indicated by the gate status $\sum_{g \in G} oc_g = U$ or the planned starting time has not passed yet, the truck remains at the parking lot ($pos_{i'} = parking\_lot$) and no further events are generated. Here, oc_g refers to the status of gate g and takes the value 1 if the gate is occupied and 0, otherwise. If both the starting time has been reached and any gate is currently unoccupied ($\min_g oc_g = 0$), the truck position of the truck is set to that gate and the event of type $e = III$ *Unload parcel from inbound truck* is added to the event list. The impact of the event on the system is illustrated in Algorithm 7.1.

Algorithm 7.1: Event: Arriving inbound truck

Input: $ST(t^c)$, $EL(t^c)$, $PA(t^c)$, inbound i', $pos_{i'}$, $start^*_{i'}$, oc_g
Output: $ST(t^n)$, $EL(t^n)$, $PA(t^c)$

1 set simulation time t^c to $at_{i'}$
2 remove current event e from $EL(t^c)$
3 **if** $t^n \geq start^*_{i'}$ **then**
4   **if** $\sum_{g \in G} oc_g = U$ **then**
5       $pos_{i'} := parking\_lot$
6   add i to $PA(t^c)$

7   **else**
8   select free gate g
9   update position $pos_{i'} := g$
10   update gate status $oc_g := 1$
11   add event of type $e' = III$ to $EL(t^c)$ with $t^{e'} = t^n$

12 **else**
13   add event of type $e' = I$ to $EL(t^c)$ with $t^{e'} := start^*_{i'}$
14 set new system state $ST(t^n) := ST(t^c)$
15 set new event list $EL(t^n) := EL(t^c)$
16 sort $EL(t^n)$ according to event times in non-descending order

---

A.2. Departing inbound truck

Once the unloading status $load_{i'}$ of an inbound truck i' reaches the value zero, the truck is fully unloaded and leaves the gate. Then, the event e^{II} *Departing inbound truck* is triggered at time t^{II}. First, we check if any inbound truck is currently waiting at the parking lot. In case only one inbound truck waits at the parking lot, it is directly assigned to the newly unoccupied gate. If more than one inbound truck is situated at the parking lot, the next inbound is chosen according to the scheduling policy. In both cases, the event *Unload parcel from inbound truck* is added to the event list. Should the parking lot be empty, no new events are generated. The resulting system state change is shown in Algorithm 7.2.

Algorithm 7.2: Event: Departing inbound truck

Input: $ST(t^c)$, $EL(t^c)$, current gate g
Output: $ST(t^n)$, $EL(t^n)$

1 set simulation time t^c to t^e
2 remove current event e from $EL(t^c)$
3 **if** $|PA(t^c)| = 1$ **then**
4 | select only inbound i' currently in $PA(t^c)$
5 | update position $pos_{i'} := g$
6 | update gate status $oc_g := 1$
7 | update parking lot status $PA(t^c) := \varnothing$
8 | add event of type $e' = III$ to $EL(t^c)$ with $t^{e'} = t^n$

9 **else if** $|PA(t^c)| > 1$ **then**
10 | select inbound i from $PA(t^c)$ according to scheduling policy
11 | update position $pos_{i'} := g$
12 | update gate status $oc_g = 1$
13 | remove i' from $PA(t^c)$
14 | add event of type $e' = III$ to $EL(t^c)$ with $t^{e'} = t^n$

15 set new system state $ST(t^n):=ST(t^c)$
16 set new event list $EL(t^n):=EL(t^c)$
17 sort $EL(t^n)$ according to event times in non-descending order

---

A.3. Unload parcel from inbound truck

In case an event of type $e = III$ *Unload parcel from inbound truck* is triggered, we first check the unloading status $load_{i'}$ of the current inbound truck i' associated with the event. In case the truck is empty ($load_{i'} = 0$), the event *Departing inbound truck* is added to the event list. Should any parcels remain in the truck ($load_{i'} > 0$), we then check if the conveyor k the parcel is designated for is currently blocked. If conveyor k is blocked ($conv_k = r_k$), the event list is scanned for the next time a parcel leaves the conveyor which corresponds to a *Load parcel to outbound truck* event. A new event of type $e = III$ *Unload parcel from inbound truck* is then generated for that point in time. In case the conveyor's capacity is not fully used, the current number of parcels on the conveyor is increased by one and the current number of parcels in the inbound truck is reduced by one. The position of parcel p is updated. Further, the events *Unload parcel from inbound truck* and *Load parcel to outbound truck* are added to the event list corresponding to the next parcel being unloaded from the inbound truck and the current parcel leaving the conveyor. The time t^e of the next event of type *Unload parcel from inbound truck* is determined using the current time and unloading duration of the parcel dp_p. The duration of the unloading process depends on the scheduling policy. It can either be a fixed value for all trucks or depend on the results of the optimization model the scheduling policy is based on. The event time of the *Load parcel to outbound truck* event is set according to the travel time $t_{i'o}$. The event is illustrated in Algorithm 7.3.

Algorithm 7.3: Event: Unload parcel from inbound truck

Input: $ST(t^c)$, $EL(t^c)$, current parcel p
Output: $ST(t^n)$, $EL(t^n)$
1   set simulation time t^c to time t^e of the current event
2   remove current event e from $EL(t^c)$
3   determine inbound i' parcel p is currently loaded on
4   determine designated conveyor k for parcel p
5   **if** $load_{i'} = 0$ **then**
6     $\lfloor$ add event $\bar{e}'$ of type $e = II$ to $EL(t^c)$ with $t^{e'} := t^n$

7   **else**
8   **if** $conv_k = r_k$ **then**
9   search $EL(t^c)$ for next event $\bar{e}$ of type $e = III$ for conveyor k
10       $\lfloor$ add event of type $e = IV$ to $EL(t^c)$ with $t^{e'} = t^{\bar{e}}$

11   **else**
12   update conveyor utilization $conv_k := conv_k + 1$
13   update parcel position $pos_p := k$
14   update loading status $load_{i'} := load_{i'} - 1$
15   determine unloading duration dp_p from scheduling policy
16   add event e'' of type $e = III$ to $EL(t^c)$ with $t^{e''} = t^c + dp_p$
17   add event e''' of type $e = IV$ to $EL(t^c)$ with $t^{e'''} = t^c + t_{i'o}$

18   set new system state $ST(t^n) = ST(t^c)$
19   set new event list $EL(t^n) = EL(t^c)$
20   sort $EL(t^n)$ according to event times in non-descending order

---

A.4. Load parcel to outbound truck

Once a parcel p reaches its designated outbound truck o, the parcel is loaded to the outbound truck in the event *Load parcel to outbound truck*. The current number of parcels on conveyor k is reduced by one and the loading status of the outbound $load_o$ is increased by one. The pseudocode of the procedure is shown in Algorithm 7.4

Algorithm 7.4: Event: Load parcel to outbound truck

Input: $ST(t^c)$, $EL(t^c)$, current parcel p
Output: $ST(t^n)$, $EL(t^n)$
1 set simulation time t^c to time t^e of the current event e' of type $e = IV$
2 remove current event e' from $EL(t^c)$
3 determine designated conveyor k and outbound o for parcel p
4 update loading status $load_o := load_o + 1$
5 update conveyor utilization $conv_k := conv_k - 1$
6 set new system state $ST(t^n) = ST(t^c)$
7 set new event list $EL(t^n) = EL(t^c)$

B. Homogenization scheme for parcel flows

To generate homogeneous parcel flows for the simulation model as a reference, a homogenization scheme that evenly distributes the parcels with regard to their destinations in the parcel unloading sequence can be applied. The homogenization scheme is shown in Algorithm 7.5.

Algorithm 7.5: Parcel flow homogenization

Input: inbound i' with $ship_{i'o}$, $b_{i'}$, conveyor assignment O_k
Output: homogenized unloading sequence seq
1 initialize empty sequence $seq^l = \{\}$
2 initialize relative number of parcels for conveyor k

$$pc_k := \frac{\sum_{o \in O_k} ship_{i'o}}{\sum_o ship_{i'o}}$$

3 initialize relative number of parcels for outbound o

$$pu_o := \frac{ship_{i'o}}{\sum_o ship_{i'o}}$$

4 **while** $|seq^l| < b_i$ **do**
5   pick $k' \in K$ with largest relative number of parcels $pc_{k'}$
6   pick $o' \in O_{k'}$ with largest relative number of parcels $pu_{o'}$
7   add o' to seq^l
8   update remaining parcels $ship_{i'o'} := ship_{i'o'} - 1$
9   update relative number of parcels for $pc_{k'}$ and $pu_{o'}$

The basic idea of the approach is to first initialize an empty unloading sequence seq^l for the inbound truck i and then iteratively add a single new parcel to the sequence. In more detail, we first calculate the fraction of remaining parcels for every conveyor with regard to the total number of parcels for that specific conveyor pc_k. The same concept is applied for the relative number of parcels for the outbounds with pu_o. In each iteration a parcel is then added according to the relative distribution of parcels for the individual conveyors by picking a parcel for the conveyor k' with currently the highest share of designated parcels pc_k. Among the outbounds $O_{k'}$ connected to k' we again select the outbound o' that has the highest relative number of parcels pu_o and add it to the sequence seq^l. At the end of each iteration, the relative number of parcels for conveyors and outbounds is updated. The algorithm stops once all parcels have been added to the sequence.

© 2023, Stefan Bugow
Herstellung und Verlag: BoD – Books on
Demand, Norderstedt
ISBN: 9783734711831